AWAKEN

DESPERTAR

DAHLIA QUIÑONEZ

DEDICATION

First, I want to dedicate this book to God, who enlightened me throughout this process and to my beautiful family, and last but not least, to my dear mother, Panchita.

I also want to dedicate this book to all my people in Latin America. They were my inspiration to write this book. My wish is that my message reaches every one of them. We cannot eradicate the poverty that exists in Latin America, but we can improve our quality of life and attitude toward life. That's what I want to say to all of them, and I hope this book can help them see things from a different perspective.

CONTENT

ACKNOWLEDGMENTS

I want to give thanks to God for making this book possible and for making me the person I am today. I express my gratitude to everyone who helped and supported me in writing this book. My friends and everyone who has helped me grow stronger by teaching me something through life's lessons.

Introduction

I decided to write this book to share what I learned in 2020 that changed my life forever. I learned beautiful things that helped me mature as a person and in my interpersonal relationships. It's about emotional traumas. It could be overwhelming to learn about psychology because there is a clinical language that people might find difficult to understand. For this reason, I want to share what I learned in the simplest way and in which everyone can understand. First, I'm not a psychologist or anything like that; I just want to share this information to help others who may be in the same situation that I was in and don't know yet. Everything I tell you in this book, I tell you from my own experience, and I am sure it will help you. These pages are full of events that have happened to me; I write these lines from what I have already experienced. I'm not talking about someone else's experience; I can only tell you about myself.

I believe psychology should be taught in elementary school since it is an essential part of human beings because our thoughts can make or break us. Learning how certain traumatic situations we have been through have shaped and affected us will change our lives forever.

In this book, I explain everything about the different psychological disorders and traumas I learned about. I present it to you in the simplest way possible.

I want to share everything I learned and how it changed my life to help others to awaken emotionally and psychologically. What do I mean when I say awaken? You will learn things in this book that will make you a self-conscientious person, aware of what happens inside of you and around you. What does it mean to be a self-conscious person? You can answer that question for yourself when you finish reading this book. You may think you don't need to learn anything since your life is more normal than anyone else. Well, think again.

But let me tell you an interesting fact, many psychologists and thinking people in this world, in their talks and books, will always quote passages from the Bible. The Bible is a divinely inspired book and the most widely distributed book in the world. I have read the Bible three times and am on my fourth reading. For my part, I can tell you that what the Bible says about a person's feelings is very powerful. An example is Proverbs 4:23, which says, "above all the things that you guard, safeguard your heart, for out of it are the sources of life." This refers to our feelings, motives, desires, and emotions because if we are not psychologically well, we can't live "normal" and happy lives. We must protect our hearts from negative thoughts, hence our creator's warning to safeguard our hearts.

For example, people with depression and other mental illnesses live as if a gray cloud hangs over them all the time. They don't live their life with pleasure. The saddest thing is that many people live with depression and don't even know they have it. They think that the life they lead is normal and almost always question the symptoms of the disease. They wonder: why don't I feel like going out and having fun? Why am I tired all the time? Why am I not happy?

Another example is people who live with personality disorders and don't know it; they ask why everything goes wrong for them? Why can't I be successful? Why am I not so fortunate in love? And even why can't I be a normal person? They live asking questions like this. If you are such a person or know someone with these types of problems, then this book can help you change your life once and for all.

If something you read in this book is happening in your life, I invite you to read it several times and meditate on it to fully understand it. That's what will help change your life, being aware of what is happening and changing it. In the index, I leave you the names of the books, encyclopedias, psychologists' names, and YouTube channels that helped me find this information. I invite you to visit each of the references as they will help you understand more deeply everything I tell you in this book.

Sharing my life and the things that happened to me over the years is not very pleasant; believe me, it makes me feel vulnerable. But I only do it to help, and I sincerely hope it is so. Feeling vulnerable is not as bad as it seems once you have healed emotionally, you will be able to see that.

CHAPTER 1
MY JOURNEY BEGINS

My journey begins in the year 2020. This year changed the lives of all people. There will always be a before and after in our lives from 2020. It was a period that marked the lives of many people. The pandemic brought much suffering, disease, and fatalities. But it was a decisive year in my life and transformation.

I never imagined that my journey would begin this year. It was the year 2020, and many of us didn't know what awaited us. I was leading a "normal" life with my husband and children in Southern California like any other family. My two older daughters live apart, and my youngest son lives with my husband and me. When the children were small, my husband and I worked, and they went to school. We took vacations every year like any other family.

Until that moment, I had no idea what I was experiencing. I have had depression for many years, which is very common nowadays. I suffered from insomnia, but who doesn't?

The year 2020 was the best year of my life. But not in the way you might imagine. For many, that year brought them a lot of suffering, and I respect their pain. For me, it meant a new beginning and opportunity in life, and maybe for you, too, after you read this book. I explain throughout the book how this came to be for me.

That year I asked God several times from the bottom of my heart to change me as a person, to change my mind, because I couldn't do it, that this was something that only he could do. I told him, "Please take out the chip in my brain and put in a new one." I knew something wasn't right, but I couldn't give it a name, and I was tired of living like that. When the quarantine began, I was devastated. I was not going to be able to do the things that until then had helped me cope with the situation I was facing, and I had no idea.

Suddenly, during the quarantine, I began finding information about my situation. I remember listening to the famous Mexican doctor Dr. Cesar Lozano and his interviews on his radio show "Por el Placer de Vivir" (For the Pleasure of Living) on Friday evenings while driving. I thank God for putting him on my path, literally. I would only listen for a few minutes, but I liked the interviews. Everything they said made a lot of sense and resonated with me. That helped me to start looking for information related to psychology. Little by little, his and other related videos began appearing on my YouTube feed during the quarantine. With everything I was learning, I realized that, in reality, my journey didn't start in the year 2020. But instead, it began in my mother's womb with her fears and anxieties and certain situations in my childhood that, until that moment, I was unaware, had marked me. What were they? They are psychological traumas. Specifically, abandonment, negligence, dependency, and narcissism. Later I will explain in more detail what these traumas are about. But how can a psychological trauma affect a child? How can having been abandoned by their parents affect a child psychologically? That was my case, but what effect does it have during childhood and later adulthood? As if the trauma we have experienced was a tattoo on our body.

When I was approximately 5 years old

Different types of traumas can affect a person's life. In the following chapter, I will tell you what those traumas are. They affect our life negatively. For now, you must understand that traumatic experiences in your life changed you without you realizing it. This made a dent in your personality and transformed it into a *Personality Disorder*. Most people in the world have experienced a traumatic event in their lifetime, so they may have a personality disorder. Sure, not everyone was affected to that point, but maybe you know someone that was.

Only after you read that disorder's description will you realize if you have it or if you have some of those personality traits. You might say, "that person described there is me." You will think, "not even I knew myself so well," which was my case, or perhaps you will say, "I know a person with the same personality." The funny thing is that people with the same personality disorder have the same behavior. No matter where they are from or if a person lives in Asia, Europe, or the American Continent. They act the same way, even though they live in different parts of the world and have different cultures. How can this be possible? Well, we all have a brain, and it works similarly. Learning how people with these disorders behave will help you to know how to deal with them, understand them and then get away from them if necessary.

But what is a personality disorder? Before we look at the description of the disorders, I want you to know the types of traumas that lead a person to develop a personality disorder. Let's see them in the next chapter.

CHAPTER 2
TRAUMAS THAT CHANGE YOUR LIFE

During our lives, we have been through traumatizing situations. We may have those experiences engraved into our minds, but what is trauma? Such a short word but so profound. How does trauma affect us to the point of destroying our lives? And why do some end up destroying the lives of others because of trauma in their lives? Why do we see mass shootings in one place after another? Why is there sexual abuse? Why do parents destroy their children's lives through alcohol, pornography, absent parenting, and destructive behavior when we know they are the ones who have to take care of them?

Next, I will leave you descriptions of common traumas. Although there are many more that a person can go through, it can be something as simple as a parent not picking up their child from school on time or a car accident. But let's look at the description of trauma.

Definition of Trauma
According to the Health Movement in California (SanaMente.org), the word **trauma** derives from the Greek language and means **wound**. A more exact definition is that

trauma is a lasting injury caused by various situations.

When we hear about traumas, we associate them with problems caused by major natural disasters such as earthquakes or hurricanes. Also, those caused by man, such as wars, accidents, etc. We can also define trauma as a strong negative emotion or impression that causes lasting damage.

A trauma arises either because you have recently suffered a fear of great intensity (terror) or because you have felt unable to handle a real or potential danger. The importance of suffering traumas during childhood and adolescence, such as any type of abuse, physical, emotional, and/or sexual, domestic violence, or suicide of a loved one, etc., is that they can lead to mental and chronic physical disorders. They affect survivors for the rest of their lives. In fact, some studies show that suffering traumas during childhood and/or adolescence is the factor that mostly contributes to the early onset of mental illnesses such as depression, anxiety, substance abuse, etc. (Sanamente.org).

Let's look at the different traumas individually to better understand them.

Trauma by Physical Abuse
Trauma by Sexual Abuse
Trauma by Psychological or Emotional Abuse
Post-Traumatic Stress Trauma
Trauma by Emotional Abandonment

Trauma by Physical Abuse
Physical abuse is any intentional act causing injury or trauma to another person or animal by way of bodily contact. In most cases, children are the victims of physical abuse, but adults can also be victims, as in cases of domestic violence or workplace aggression. Physical abuse means any non-accidental act or behavior causing

injury, trauma, or other physical suffering or bodily harm. Abusive acts toward children can often result from parents' attempts at child discipline through excessive corporal punishment.

Physically abused children are at risk for later interpersonal problems involving aggressive behavior, and adolescents are at a much greater risk for substance use disorders. In addition, symptoms of depression, emotional distress, and suicidal ideation are also common features of people who have been physically abused. As many as one-third of children who experience physical abuse are also at risk to become abusive as adults (wikipedia.org).

Trauma by Sexual Abuse

Any request or exercise of contact, caresses, games, or touching, in which at least one of those involved does not want, knows, or lacks awareness of what is happening and that is obtained by force or descent with the victim. (García Morey, 2008)

The psychological consequences that have been related to the experience of childhood sexual abuse can last throughout the evolutionary cycle and configure, in adulthood, the so-called long-term effects of sexual abuse. It is also possible that the victim does not develop apparent problems during childhood and that these appear as new problems in adulthood.

There is talk of long-term effects when they occur two years after the experience of abuse, occurring in approximately 20% of victims of child sexual abuse.

The long-term effects are comparatively less frequent than the initial consequences; however, childhood sexual abuse constitutes an important risk factor for the development of a wide variety of psychopathological disorders in adulthood. The information currently available does not allow us to establish a single specific syndrome, or set of differentiated symptoms, associated with the experience of sexual abuse at this vital stage, affecting different areas of the victim's life; just as it does not allow us to confirm the existence of a linear relationship between the experience of child sexual abuse and the presence of psychological problems in adulthood, multiple variables seem to affect this relationship. The long-term effects of child sexual abuse have been considered speculative, highlighting the difficulty involved in their study, especially when compared with the initial consequences, and mainly given their interaction with other types of factors related to the passage of time (López, 1993).

The main psychological consequences found are grouped into five categories: emotional problems, relationship problems, functional problems, adjustment problems, and sexual problems (www.pepsic.vbsalud.org/scielo).

Consequences derived from sexual violence:
The consequences largely depend on the type of abuse and your circumstances. Studies estimate that a high percentage of the victims of Violence or Sexual Abuse present sequels, among which are: mistrust, fear, hostility towards the sex of the person who attacked or towards the family if they feel that they did not protect themselves, shame, anxiety, guilt, running away from home, school failure and drug use, high incidence of sexual dissatisfaction and dysfunction, depression, anxiety, increased incidence of unwanted pregnancies and early pregnancy, early initiation of sexual relations and sexually transmitted infections.
The consequences are usually greater the more emotionally close the person who attacked is, the more violence there has been, the longer it has taken place, and the less the victim has been believed in and/or supported (www.svet.gob.gt).

Post-Traumatic Stress Trauma

Post-traumatic stress disorder (PTSD) is a mental health disorder that some people develop after they experience or see a traumatic event. The traumatic event may be life-threatening, such as combat, a natural disaster, a car accident, or sexual assault. But sometimes the event is not necessarily a dangerous one. For example, the sudden, unexpected death of a loved one can also cause PTSD.

It's normal to feel afraid during and after a traumatic situation. The fear triggers a "fight-or-flight" response. This is your body's way of helping to protect itself from possible harm. It causes changes in your body such as the release of certain hormones and increases in alertness, blood pressure, heart rate, and breathing.

In time, most people recover from this naturally. But people with PTSD don't feel better. They feel stressed and frightened long after the trauma is over. In some cases, the PTSD symptoms may start later on. They might also come and go over time.

You can develop PTSD at any age. Many risk factors play a part in whether you will develop PTSD. They include:

> Your sex; women are more likely to develop PTSD
> Having had trauma in childhood
> Feeling horror, helplessness, or extreme fear
> Going through a traumatic event that lasts a long time
> Having little or no social support after the event
> Dealing with extra stress after the event, such as loss of a loved one, pain and injury, or loss of a job or home
> Having a history of mental illness or substance use

There are four types of PTSD symptoms, but they may not be the same for everyone. Each person experiences symptoms in their own way. The types are:

Re-experiencing symptoms, where something reminds you of the trauma and you feel that fear again. Examples include:

> Flashbacks, which cause you to feel like you are going through the event again
>
> Nightmares
>
> Frightening thoughts

Avoidance symptoms, where you try to avoid situations or people that trigger memories of the traumatic event. This may cause you to

> Stay away from places, events, or objects that are reminders of the traumatic experience. For example, if you were in a car accident, you might stop driving.
>
> Avoiding thoughts or feelings related to the traumatic event. For example, you might try to stay very busy to try to avoid thinking about what happened.

Arousal and reactivity symptoms, which may cause you to be jittery or be on the lookout for danger. They include

> Being easily startled
>
> Feeling tense or "on edge"
>
> Having difficulty sleeping
>
> Having angry outbursts

Cognition and mood symptoms, which are negative changes in beliefs and feelings. They include

> Trouble remembering important things about the traumatic event
>
> Negative thoughts about yourself or the world
>
> Feeling blame and guilt
>
> No longer being interested in things you enjoyed
>
> Trouble concentrating

The symptoms usually start soon after the traumatic event. But sometimes they may not appear until months or years later. They also may come and go over many years (medlineplus.gov).

Trauma by Psychological or Emotional Abuse

Psychological abuse, often called emotional abuse, is a form of abuse characterized by a person subjecting or exposing another person to a behavior that may result in psychological trauma, including anxiety, chronic depression, or post-traumatic stress disorder.

It is often associated with situations of power imbalance in abusive relationships, and may include bullying, gaslighting, and abuse in the workplace. It also may be perpetrated by persons conducting torture, other violence, acute or prolonged human rights abuse, particularly without legal redress such as detention without trial, false accusations, false convictions, and extreme defamation such as were perpetrated by state and media. More specifically, "emotional abuse is any kind of abuse that is emotional rather than physical in nature. It can include anything from verbal abuse and constant criticism to more subtle tactics such as intimidation, manipulation, and refusal to ever be pleased. This abuse occurs when someone says words or does actions used to try and control the other person, to keep the other afraid and instill fear that, or kept apart from others or try to break someone's self-esteem of themselves.

Emotional abuse can take several forms. Three general patterns of abusive behavior include aggressing, denying, and minimizing"; "Withholding is another form of denying. Withholding includes refusing to listen, refusing to communicate, and emotionally withdrawing as punishment." Even though there is no established definition for emotional abuse, emotional abuse can possess a definition beyond verbal and psychological abuse. Blaming, shaming, and name calling are a few verbally abusive behaviors which can affect a victim emotionally. The victim's self-worth and emotional well-being are altered and even diminished by the verbal abuse, resulting in an emotionally-abused victim.

Prevalence

Intimate relationships
When discussing the different types of psychological abuse in terms of domestically violent relationships, it is important to recognize the 4 different types; Denigrating Damage to Partner's Self-Image or Esteem, Passive Aggressive Withholding of Emotional Support, Threatening Behavior, and Restricting Personal Territory and Freedom.

Child Emotional Abuse
Psychological abuse of a child is commonly defined as a pattern of behavior by parents or caregivers that can seriously interfere with a child's cognitive, emotional, psychological, or social development. According to the DSM-5, Child Psychological Abuse is defined as verbal or symbolic acts given by parent or caregiver which can result in significant psychological harm. Examples are yelling, comparing to others, name-calling, blaming, gaslighting, manipulating, and normalizing abuse due to the status of being underage.

Some parents may emotionally and psychologically harm their children because of stress, poor parenting skills, social isolation, and lack of available resources or inappropriate expectations of their children (wikipedia.org)

Trauma by Emotional Abandonment
Emotional abandonment is a subjective emotional state in which people feel undesired, left behind, insecure, or discarded. People experiencing emotional abandonment may feel at a loss. They may feel like they have been cut off from a crucial source of sustenance or feel withdrawn, either suddenly or through a process of erosion. Emotional abandonment can manifest through loss or separation from a loved one.

Feeling rejected, which is a significant component of emotional abandonment which has a biological impact in that it activates the physical pain centers of the brain and can leave an emotional imprint in the brain's warning system.

Individuals who experience feelings of emotional abandonment are likely to also experience maladaptive thoughts ("irrational beliefs") and behaviors such as depressive symptoms and relationship avoidance and/or dependence. This may cause abundant difficulty in daily life with interpersonal relationships and social settings. Feelings of emotional abandonment can stem from numerous situations. While such maladaptive thoughts and behaviors are sometimes present in the context of certain psychological disorders (e.g., borderline personality disorder, antisocial personality disorder, depression, anxiety disorders), not all individuals who experience feelings of emotional abandonment will meet criteria for such a psychological disorders. These individuals may function within normal limits in spite of the presence of these emotional difficulties (wikipedia.org).

These are some of the different types of traumas. Now that we know what traumas are and their descriptions, let's look at the consequences of the traumas on people in the next chapter.

Now you are thinking, what good is it for me to learn all the clinical terms and those things? If you want to be awakened, there is no other way; there are no shortcuts. Now let's see the consequence of traumas on human beings.

CHAPTER 3
CONSEQUENCES OF THE TRAUMAS

What are the consequences of the traumas we experimented with? Some of them let us to develop a personality disorder. But what is a personality disorder?

First, let's look at the definition of a personality disorder.

Personality Disorder Description
A personality disorder is a type of mental disorder in which you have a rigid and unhealthy pattern of thinking, functioning, and behaving. A person with a personality disorder has trouble perceiving and relating to situations and people. This causes significant problems and limitations in relationships, social activities, work, and school.

In some cases, you may not realize that you have a personality disorder because your way of thinking and behaving seems natural to you. And you may blame others for the challenges you face.

Personality disorders usually begin in the teenage years or early adulthood. There are many types of personality disorders. Some types may become less obvious throughout middle age. (mayoclinic.org).

The causes can be genetic or the environment we grew up in. If your mother or father was diagnosed with a mental illness, it might be passed on to their children. Also, a one-time traumatic event like an accident, sexual abuse, being emotionally abused throughout our life, negligence, or any other traumatic events will lead a person to develop a personality disorder.

Next, I will list the different personality disorders for you. You must familiarize yourself with them to understand what I'm talking about in the book. While reading the descriptions, you might see yourself reflected on them or see someone else there. Reading each description will help you understand why a person behaves or acts a certain way. It will also help you in your interpersonal relationships, for example, with your family, work, school, and other aspects of your life. Because you will know exactly how to deal with those that have personality disorders. If you learn what personality disorders are, you can also help others that have the disorder and don't even know it.

It should be noted that even if a person has one type of disorder, they may also have traits of another. Many may have symptoms and signs of other disorders. For example, someone may have narcissistic traits but will also have dependent or co-dependent traits. I identify myself with this.

Here is a list of the different personality disorders. Make sure you see if there are any traits of your personality in any of them.

Personality Disorders

Paranoid Personality Disorder
Schizoid Personality Disorder
Schizotypal Personality Disorder
Antisocial Personality Disorder
Borderline Personality Disorder
Histrionic Personality Disorder
Narcissistic Personality Disorder

Avoidant Personality Disorder
Dependent Personality Disorder
Obsessive-compulsive Personality Disorder

Paranoid Personality Disorder
Paranoid personality disorder (PPD) is a mental condition in which a person has a long-term pattern of distrust and suspicion of others. The person does not have a full-blown psychotic disorder, such as schizophrenia. The causes of PPD are unknown. PPD seems to be more common in families with psychotic disorders, such as schizophrenia and delusional disorder. This suggests genes may be involved. Other factors may play a role as well. PPD seems to be more common in men.

People with PPD are very suspicious of other people. As a result, they severely limit their social lives. They often feel that they are in danger and look for evidence to support their suspicions. They have trouble seeing that their distrust is out of proportion to their environment.

Common symptoms include:
Concern that other people have hidden motives
Thinking that they will be exploited (used) or harmed by others
Not able to work together with others
Social isolation
Detachment
Hostility
(medlineplus.gov)

   You can imagine the life of a person with a paranoid personality disorder. When someone lives without trust, they live an unhappy life. The person lives with mistrust and doubting everything and everybody. They can't talk and express their feelings freely because they think people will use what they say against them. Their lives are very miserable, and they don't even know it. They take everything personally, thinking that people are always talking about and insulting them, making them live bitter lives. Always imputing bad motives to other people will only cause them to live resentfully. But what hurts the person the most is to harvest resentfulness. Having feelings of resentfulness only hurts us. Because the person that did something to us may not even know the other one is holding grudges against them unless the other person tells them. This reminds me of what Nelson Mandela said: "Resentment is like drinking poison and then hoping it will kill your enemies."

The person with Paranoid Personality disorder is living this way of life without knowing it is a personality disorder. He might think that this is normal and that he acts like that because of the bad experiences in life. He will even justify himself by saying, "I wasn't like that; they made me." He thinks that behaving in such a way is the right thing to do because it will protect them from being harmed by others.

Schizoid Personality Disorder

Schizoid personality disorder is an uncommon condition in which people avoid social activities and consistently shy away from interaction with others. They also have a limited range of emotional expression. If you have schizoid personality disorder, you may be seen as a loner or dismissive of others, and you may lack the desire or skill to form close personal relationships. Because you don't tend to show emotion, you may appear as though you don't care about others or what's going on around you. The cause of schizoid personality disorder is unknown.

Symptoms: Prefer being alone and choose to do activities alone, don't want or enjoy close relationships, feel little if any desire for sexual relationships, feel like you can't experience pleasure, have difficulty expressing emotions and reacting appropriately to situations, may seem humorless, indifferent or emotionally cold to others, may appear to lack motivation and goals and don't react to praise or critical remarks from others

Schizoid personality disorder usually begins by early adulthood, though some features may be noticeable during childhood. These features may cause you to have trouble functioning well in school, a job, or in other areas of life. However, you may do reasonably well in your job if you mostly work alone (mayoclinic.org).

Persons with this type of personality disorder are usually very quiet and give the impression of not giving importance to different situations. They are not interested in social activities. They find no pleasure in doing things even though they feel happy when they do them because they refuse to be happy. It is sad to live the life of a person with this personality disorder without anything that can make them happy. You can identify a person with this disorder when you see no emotions in their face. They have a "poker face," as they call it in the poker game, because you will see no facial expression in different situations.

Schizotypal Personality Disorder

People with schizotypal personality disorder are often described as odd or eccentric and usually have few if any, close relationships. They generally don't understand how relationships form or the impact of their behavior on others. They may also misinterpret others' motivations and behaviors and develop a significant distrust of others. These problems may lead to severe anxiety and a tendency to avoid social situations, as the person with schizotypal personality disorder tends to hold peculiar beliefs and may have difficulty responding appropriately to social cues. Schizotypal personality disorder typically is diagnosed in early adulthood and is likely to endure across the lifespan, though treatment, such as medications and therapy, can improve symptoms.

Schizotypal personality disorder typically includes five or more of these signs and symptoms: being a loner and lacking close friends outside of the immediate family, flat emotions or limited or inappropriate emotional responses, persistent and excessive social anxiety, incorrect interpretation of events, such as a feeling that something that is actually harmless or inoffensive has a direct personal meaning, peculiar, eccentric or unusual thinking, beliefs or mannerisms, suspicious or paranoid thoughts and constant doubts about the loyalty of others, belief in special powers, such as mental telepathy or superstitions, unusual perceptions, such as sensing an absent person's presence or having illusions, dressing in peculiar ways, such as appearing unkempt or wearing oddly matched clothes and peculiar style of speech, such as vague or unusual patterns of speaking, or rambling oddly during conversations (mayoclinic.org).

During your life, you will encounter a person with this personality disorder. This type of person doesn't have many friends because he has problems relating to others. Now and then, they will tell you how certain events were revealed to them before they happened. You might think they are kidding, but they are not, they are serious about it. They think they have a certain influence on events that are about to happen. You will also recognize them by their very particular way of dressing. When we are young, we dress fashionably and sometimes rebelliously. However, when a person has passed their younger years and is still dressing a certain way, you will know that the person has a problem.

Antisocial Personality Disorder

Antisocial personality disorder, sometimes called sociopathy, is a mental disorder in which a person consistently shows no regard for right and wrong and ignores the rights and feelings of others. People with antisocial personality disorder tend to antagonize, manipulate or treat others harshly or with callous indifference. They show no guilt or remorse for their behavior.

Individuals with antisocial personality disorder often violate the law, becoming criminals. They may lie, behave violently or impulsively, and have problems with drug and alcohol use. Because of these characteristics, people with this disorder typically can't fulfill responsibilities related to family, work or school.

Symptoms:

Disregard for right and wrong

Persistent lying or deceit to exploit others

Being callous, cynical and disrespectful of others

Using charm or wit to manipulate others for personal gain or personal pleasure

Arrogance, a sense of superiority and being extremely opinionated

Recurring problems with the law, including criminal behavior

Repeatedly violating the rights of others through intimidation and dishonesty

Impulsiveness or failure to plan ahead

Hostility, significant irritability, agitation, aggression or violence

Lack of empathy for others and lack of remorse about harming others

Unnecessary risk-taking or dangerous behavior with no regard for the safety of self or others

Poor or abusive relationships

Failure to consider the negative consequences of behavior or learn from them

Being consistently irresponsible and repeatedly failing to fulfill work or financial obligations

Adults with antisocial personality disorder typically show symptoms of conduct disorder before the age of 15. Signs and symptoms of conduct disorder include serious, persistent behavior problems, such as:

Aggression toward people and animals

Destruction of property

Deceitfulness
Theft
Serious violation of rules

Although antisocial personality disorder is considered lifelong, in some people, certain symptoms — particularly destructive and criminal behavior — may decrease over time. But it's not clear whether this decrease is a result of aging or an increased awareness of the consequences of antisocial behavior (mayoclinic.org).

You will see persons with this personality disorder misbehaving very often, on the streets, at work, at school, and everywhere you go. You might think, how can that person be so irresponsible? How can he be such a bad person? Later, I will explain how the person developed this personality disorder. The person doesn't know that his personality is part of a psychological disorder, so he feels no remorse for his bad behavior. The person has no moral compass. Their conscience doesn't tell them that what they are doing is wrong.

They have no regard for traffic laws or any other laws because they think they are special and those laws don't apply to them. You will find them, for example, in traffic school ranging from 16 to 65 years old because it doesn't matter how old they are. They still have the personality disorder if they haven't found out that they have the personality disorder and haven't worked on healing themselves.

Borderline Personality Disorder
Borderline personality disorder is a mental health disorder that impacts the way you think and feel about yourself and others, causing problems functioning in everyday life. It includes self-image issues, difficulty managing emotions and behavior, and a pattern of unstable relationships.

With borderline personality disorder, you have an intense fear of abandonment or instability, and you may have difficulty tolerating being alone. Yet inappropriate anger, impulsiveness and frequent mood swings may push others away, even though you want to have loving and lasting relationships. Borderline personality disorder usually begins by early adulthood. The condition seems to be worse in young adulthood and may gradually get better with age.

Symptoms:
Borderline personality disorder affects how you feel about yourself, how you relate to others and how you behave.
Signs and symptoms may include:
An intense fear of abandonment, even going to extreme measures to avoid real or imagined separation or rejection
A pattern of unstable intense relationships, such as idealizing someone one moment and then suddenly believing the person doesn't care enough or is cruel
Rapid changes in self-identity and self-image that include shifting goals and values, and seeing yourself as bad or as if you don't exist at all
Periods of stress-related paranoia and loss of contact with reality, lasting from a few minutes to a few hours
Impulsive and risky behavior, such as gambling, reckless driving, unsafe sex, spending sprees, binge eating or drug abuse, or sabotaging success by suddenly quitting a good job or ending a positive relationship
Suicidal threats or behavior or self-injury, often in response to fear of separation or rejection
Wide mood swings lasting from a few hours to a few days, which can include intense happiness, irritability, shame or anxiety
Ongoing feelings of emptiness
Inappropriate, intense anger, such as frequently losing your temper, being sarcastic or bitter, or having physical fights

If you have borderline personality disorder, don't get

discouraged. Many people with this disorder get better over time with treatment and can learn to live satisfying lives (mayoclinic.org).

The person with this disorder is always on edge, just like the disorder's name. You will see them running underground car races. They are always putting their life in danger. They feel an emptiness inside; that is why they want to fill it with the adrenaline of putting their life on the edge. They like to have love relationships where they always argue with their partner because they saw that with their parents. They can't live without those feelings of distress because being in that state of mind liberates certain endorphins in their body, and they become addicted to them.

Histrionic Personality Disorder

Histrionic personality disorder is a mental condition in which people act in a very emotional and dramatic way that draws attention to them. The causes of histrionic personality disorder are unknown. Genes and early childhood events may be responsible. It is diagnosed more often in women than in men. Doctors believe that more men may have the disorder than are diagnosed. Histrionic personality disorder usually begins by late teens or early 20s.

People with this disorder are usually able to function at a high level and can be successful socially and at work.

Symptoms include:
Acting or looking overly seductive
Being easily influenced by other people
Being overly concerned with their looks
Being overly dramatic and emotional
Being overly sensitive to criticism or disapproval
Believing that relationships are more intimate than they actually

are
Blaming failure or disappointment on others
Constantly seeking reassurance or approval
Having a low tolerance for frustration or delayed gratification
Needing to be the center of attention (self-centeredness)
Quickly changing emotions, which may seem shallow to others

People with this condition often seek treatment when they have depression or anxiety from failed romantic relationships or other conflicts with people (medlineplus.gov).

You will recognize this type of person because they want to have all the attention of others; they love to be the center of attention. They are fanciful and naive. They could go from sad to happy in an instant. They always have to be part of a group. They always have to use the word "us" and not "me" because they fear rejection and abandonment. Their fears will lead them to make decisions that are not in their best interest because they don't want to be alone.

Histrionics are chosen by persons with a narcissistic personality disorder to be their partners because they rather choose to be with someone that mistreats them than end up alone. The narcissist takes advantage of this. The histrionic will live forever grateful to the narcissist for choosing him and being part of a group. The histrionic person considers all his interpersonal relationships to be very close or intimate even if they are not, but they are in their minds.

Narcissistic Personality Disorder

Narcissistic personality disorder is a mental health condition in which people have an unreasonably high sense of their own importance. They need and seek too much attention and want people to admire them. People with this disorder may lack the ability to understand or care about the feelings of others. But behind this mask of extreme confidence, they are not sure of their self-worth and are easily upset by the slightest criticism. A narcissistic personality disorder causes problems in many areas of life, such as relationships, work, school or financial matters. People with narcissistic personality disorder may be generally unhappy and disappointed when they're not given the special favors or admiration that they believe they deserve. They may find their relationships troubled and unfulfilling, and other people may not enjoy being around them.

Narcissistic personality disorder affects more males than females, and it often begins in the teens or early adulthood. Some children may show traits of narcissism, but this is often typical for their age and doesn't mean they'll go on to develop narcissistic personality disorder.

Symptoms:
Have an unreasonably high sense of self-importance and require constant, excessive admiration.
Feel that they deserve privileges and special treatment.
Expect to be recognized as superior even without achievements.
Make achievements and talents seem bigger than they are.
Be preoccupied with fantasies about success, power, brilliance, beauty or the perfect mate.
Believe they are superior to others and can only spend time with or be understood by equally special people.
Be critical of and look down on people they feel are not important.
Expect special favors and expect other people to do what they want without questioning them.
Take advantage of others to get what they want.
Have an inability or unwillingness to recognize the needs and feelings of others.
Be envious of others and believe others envy them.
Behave in an arrogant way, brag a lot and come across as conceited.

Insist on having the best of everything — for instance, the best car or office.

At the same time, people with narcissistic personality disorder have trouble handling anything they view as criticism. They can:

> Become impatient or angry when they don't receive special recognition or treatment.
> Have major problems interacting with others and easily feel slighted.
> React with rage or contempt and try to belittle other people to make themselves appear superior.
> Have difficulty managing their emotions and behavior.
> Experience major problems dealing with stress and adapting to change.
> Withdraw from or avoid situations in which they might fail.
> Feel depressed and moody because they fall short of perfection.
> Have secret feelings of insecurity, shame, humiliation and fear of being exposed as a failure.

People with narcissistic personality disorder may not want to think that anything could be wrong, so they usually don't seek treatment. If they do seek treatment, it's more likely to be for symptoms of depression, drug or alcohol misuse, or another mental health problem. What they view as insults to self-esteem may make it difficult to accept and follow through with treatment (mayoclinic.org).

This type of personality disorder has become a silent pandemic in this century, the social media channels have helped to foment narcissistic attitudes. Later I will explain this disorder in detail and how it has affected many people. This person has a grandiose personality. He thinks highly about himself. He only loves himself. He cannot empathize with anyone, not even his relatives. In a social gathering, he wants to be the center of attention, and if he doesn't have it, he would rather leave the party.

Avoidant Personality Disorder

Avoidant personality disorder is a mental condition in which a person has a lifelong pattern of feeling very:
Shy
Inadequate
Sensitive to rejection

The causes of avoidant personality disorder are unknown. Genes or a physical illness that changed the person's appearance may play a role.

People with this disorder cannot stop thinking about their own shortcomings. They form relationships with other people only if they believe they will not be rejected. Loss and rejection are so painful that these people choose to be lonely rather than risk trying to connect with others.
A person with avoidant personality disorder may:
Be easily hurt when people criticize or disapprove of them
Hold back too much in intimate relationships
Be reluctant to become involved with people
Avoid activities or jobs that involve contact with others
Be shy in social situations out of fear of doing something wrong
Make potential difficulties seem worse than they are
Hold the view they are not good socially, not as good as other people, or unappealing

People with this disorder may develop some ability to relate to others. With treatment this can be improved (medlineplus.gov).

The person with this disorder will never look you in the eyes when they are talking to you. Do you know someone that does this?

Dependent Personality Disorder
Dependent personality disorder is a mental condition in which people depend too much on others to meet their emotional and physical needs. The causes of dependent personality disorder are unknown. The disorder usually begins in childhood. It is one of the most common personality disorders and is equally common in men and women.
People with this disorder don't trust their own ability to make decisions. They may be very upset by separation and loss. They may go to great lengths, even suffering abuse, to stay in a relationship.

Symptoms of dependent personality disorder may include:
Avoiding being alone
Avoiding personal responsibility
Becoming easily hurt by criticism or disapproval
Becoming overly focused on fears of being abandoned
Becoming very passive in relationships
Feeling very upset or helpless when relationships end
Having difficulty making decisions without support from others
Having problems expressing disagreements with others
(medlineplus.gov)

You will recognize people with dependent personalities for their romantic relationships in which their partner mistreats them. Still, they cannot leave them due to their dependency. They cannot be without a partner or someone who can care for them and always be with them. Also, they are the ideal partner for people with a narcissistic personality disorder because they will always stay in the relationship even if they mistreat them. Some people don't understand that kind of behavior. It is difficult to understand women who are mistreated by their partners and do not leave them. This happens because of their personality disorder. Once the person realizes they have it and works on it, they can leave the abusive person.

Maybe they grew up in an environment where they were made to feel like they weren't enough and were told they were dumb and couldn't do things right. Now they always need someone to help them and can't do things independently. And as I said before, even if they have a more dominant personality disorder, they have traits of other disorders. So we see repeating behaviors across the different disorders. Perhaps the person is dependent but also has narcissistic traits because they had a narcissistic parent.

Obsessive-compulsive Personality Disorder
Obsessive-compulsive personality disorder (OCPD) is a mental condition in which a person is preoccupied with:
Rules
Orderliness
Control
OCPD tends to occur in families, so genes may be involved. A person's childhood and environment may also play roles.
This disorder can affect both men and women. It occurs most often in men.
Symptoms:
OCPD has some of the same symptoms as obsessive-compulsive disorder (OCD). People with OCD have unwanted thoughts, while people with OCPD believe that their thoughts are correct. In addition, OCD often begins in childhood while OCPD usually starts in the teen years or early 20s.
People with either OCPD or OCD are high achievers and feel a sense of urgency about their actions. They may become very upset if other people interfere with their rigid routines. They may not be able to express their anger directly. People with OCPD have feelings that they consider more appropriate, like anxiety or frustration.

A person with OCPD has symptoms of perfectionism that usually begin by early adulthood. This perfectionism may interfere with the person's ability to complete tasks because their standards are so rigid. They may withdraw emotionally when they are not able to control a situation. This can interfere with their ability to solve problems and form close relationships.

Other signs of OCPD include:

Over-devotion to work

Not being able to throw things away, even when the objects have no value

Lack of flexibility

Lack of generosity

Not wanting to allow other people to do things

Not willing to show affection

Preoccupation with details, rules, and lists

The social isolation and difficulty handling anger that are common with OCPD may lead to depression and anxiety later in life (medlineplus.gov).

You will recognize people with this type of disorder by their hoarding behavior. They don't like to throw anything away; they prefer to keep it in case they need it one day. There's even a hoarder's show on TV. But they have such behavior due to their personality disorder.

Remember that these personality disorders were created in us due to traumatic events we went through in our lives, either one-time events or a series of events.

Did you identify with any of these mental disorders? What can help you heal and reverse the damage caused? First, learning about it, second, being aware that you have it and third, acceptance. Because if we deny that we have a problem, then we will never be able to fix it.

Another personality disorder that is not very common but some people suffer from is a mental disorder called Dissociative Identity Disorder. It is a disease that leads the person to transform into a different person from what they are and transform into the person they were when the trauma happened, when an event triggers the change.

Let's see the description of Dissociative Identity Disorder.

Dissociative Identity Disorder

Dissociative disorders are mental disorders that involve experiencing a disconnection and lack of continuity between thoughts, memories, surroundings, actions and identity. People with dissociative disorders escape reality in ways that are involuntary and unhealthy and cause problems with functioning in everyday life. Dissociative disorders usually develop as a reaction to trauma and help keep difficult memories at bay. Symptoms — ranging from amnesia to alternate identities — depend in part on the type of dissociative disorder you have. Times of stress can temporarily worsen symptoms, making them more obvious.

Treatment for dissociative disorders may include talk therapy (psychotherapy) and medication. Although treating dissociative disorders can be difficult, many people learn new ways of coping and lead healthy, productive lives.

Signs and symptoms depend on the type of dissociative disorders you have, but may include:

Memory loss (amnesia) of certain time periods, events, people and personal information

A sense of being detached from yourself and your emotions

A perception of the people and things around you as distorted and unreal

A blurred sense of identity

Significant stress or problems in your relationships, work or other important areas of your life

Inability to cope well with emotional or professional stress

Mental health problems, such as depression, anxiety, and suicidal thoughts and behaviors

There are three major dissociative disorders defined in the Diagnostic and Statistical Manual of Mental Disorders (DSM-5), published by the American Psychiatric Association: Dissociative amnesia, dissociative identity disorder and depersonalization-derealization disorder (mayoclinic.org).

An example of this is when the person who suffers from this disorder may suddenly see something that reminds him of the traumatizing event, which makes him go back to that time. It may be that an adult person sees or smells something that reminds them of their traumatic experience as a child. At that moment, he transforms himself into a child.

Some people can have more than ten personalities, such as a child's personality, a teenager's personality, or a different person from who they are. It's hard to believe, right? As if taken from a movie, Hollywood actually made a movie that depicts this disorder; it is called "Split," where a man with more than 23 personalities is represented. Of course, you must consider that it's a movie, and the reality may be different.

You might think this is a new disease, but it's not. You can search the internet for the HBO documentary "Multiple Personality Disorder," which shows you several cases of people with this disorder. Gretchen's case is very peculiar. Since then, more has been known about this disorder.

A more recent example would be a famous YouTuber named Encina Severa. On her YouTube channel, she has videos showing how she changes into her different personalities. She tells in interviews that she experienced many traumatizing experiences in her childhood.

Maybe you know people who suffer from this, and you haven't noticed. According to the National Alliance on Mental Illness, it is estimated that 2% of the population suffers from this disease. It may not be such a dramatic change or transformation as those presented in the movie. Still, you can notice the behaviors as those manifested.

I reiterate I only say what I have experienced and seen in other people. I experienced something similar years ago. I was glad that I realized what had happened to me and was aware of it. It happened to me around 2018, and I had not realized that it had happened to me until two years later, in 2020, when I found this information. I remembered that I had visited a place in childhood, and while there, I felt helpless. Is a place very dear to my family but where I had experienced many traumatic events. During my childhood, I suffered from child neglect. And while I was there with my aunt and nephews, I never thought about what I would eat or what we would eat for lunch. I went into my victim state of mind and became that helpless little girl I was when living there. Since in my subconscious mind, I was that little girl, and then if there wasn't anything to eat, it was okay not to eat. I was only there for two days. Two years later, remembering what had happened to me, I cried. I was sad and ashamed, especially of my aunt, because what would she have thought of me? "A grown woman, and she doesn't even worry about what she will eat? What is wrong with her?" Still writing about this brings a lump to my throat. I had turned into that neglected child when I was there and didn't even realize it. How can things like that happen? The mind is really powerful. The brain that our creator gave us is very complex.

Now that I'm aware of this and have experienced it, I have noticed some people do this, and they don't even know it. Since they don't know they have this disorder, their transformation is 100% real to them. They can behave in one way, in one place, and in a different way, in another, and it is normal for them. Only the people who live with them will notice the person's transformation. But since they don't know about this, they consider it normal.

Some people have found alternatives or not-so-conventional names for these mental disorders. Many call these disorders wounds of the soul, which makes sense to me. I will explain these wounds of the soul in the next chapter.

CHAPTER 4
THE WOUNDS

Many people have drawn conclusions about the ailments and diseases in existence. These are unconventional diagnoses but have helped many people heal, including me. You can decide whether you want to believe or not, depending on your beliefs are.

We often want to believe only what is scientific, but it is worth exploring alternatives. Personally, whatever works for me, I take, and what doesn't, I discard.

But to give you an example, Neuroscientist Caroline Leaf, Author of the book "Cleaning Up Your Mental Mess," says that we can heal from depression without medication. She says that medication only masks the pain that the person is going through and doesn't cure it. She has done research and knows what she is saying. I'm not telling you not to take medicine for depression, but to try to heal from it instead. In my case, I favor using professional help to treat mental illness. I recommend taking medication to treat whatever condition you have if you are not working on healing yourself from the inside out.

For example, when a person's kidney fails or has high cholesterol, they take medication for it. Mental illnesses cannot be seen, but they also have to be treated, and if the only way we can treat it is with medication, then; we have to take it.

The ideal thing would be to cure ourselves from the root up by taking care of our bodies so as not to depend on medication. Still, each person is different and has to do whatever is best for them.

Later I will tell you how I cured myself of depression without medication; I had depression since I was a child. The first time I went to the psychologist, I realized that I had depression when I didn't even know the word depression or what it was. I recognized that since I began to have consciousness, I have had feelings of sadness and hopelessness.

The five wounds are a concept of Lise Bourbeau, Author of the book "The Five Wounds That Prevent You from Being Yourself." She defines each one of these wounds since she was the one who discovered them after a meticulous study of the attitudes and personalities of people. She says that when each wound is activated, we put on a mask or act with certain attitudes to protect ourselves and not feel pain, this being our ego. She explains that when we are threatened, our ego comes out to protect us, putting on a mask, as she calls it.

I will give you an example; I always had a recurring painful memory of myself. I couldn't understand why. It was the day someone told me that I was an adopted child. I was about five years old. One of my cousins came to my house and said mockingly: "You already know your mom is not your real mom, right? You already know she is not your mom; your mom is someone else." I felt so bad like the whole world was crumbling down around me. Everything I knew until that moment was falling apart, but I acted like I was strong and internalized my emotions. Meditating I discovered the reason that memory came to mind. I found that this was the first time I put on a mask to avoid feeling bad. Even though I was just a little girl, I didn't cry; I only felt pain, but I became strong, or maybe my ego came out so I wouldn't feel bad. From then on, I began to use the same tactic to cover my feelings or harden my heart and not suffer.

I did what Tom Nuyens says in his "Alive Academy" seminar. I started putting on iron layers over my heart (I'll tell you about his seminar later). He says that during our lives, we are covering our hearts with these layers so that we no longer feel, and if we take them off and open our hearts again, we can heal ourselves.

In her book, Lise talks about reincarnation; I don't believe in it. I believe that our ancestors' trauma, fears, and suffering are passed on to us through our genes, and I will give you two examples of why I think this way. The first example is that when I was a child, I remember hearing about a famous Mexican television host that had undergone a kidney transplant. He said that after the surgery, he sometimes had nightmares and woke up at night dreaming he was in the middle of a shooting. Hence, he investigated whose kidney it was and found it belonged to a police officer who died in Texas. That means that the memories of that person were in his kidney.

The second example is a TV show; I like to watch a television show called "Finding your Roots," where they research the participant's family tree. They find out where they came from, their ancestors, and what they did. And every time, I can see how the ancestor's trade or line of work matches that of the participant. He had no idea that his ancestor had done the same thing before him. Again, that legacy is passed on to us through genes. But that doesn't mean that what our ancestors did we have to repeat; there is hope. Caroline Leaf says that we can change our genes. We do it by deprogramming ourselves from the attitudes our ancestors instilled in us and changing our thoughts for the better. There is a reason why the Bible says that we have to "continue to be made new in our dominant mental attitude" in Ephesians 4:23. The word "continue" denotes continuity. It means that we always have to be working on our personality. Not just once, not many times, but all our lives. Our creator is undoubtedly always right; he tells us what to do for a reason.

But without further ado, let's see what those five wounds of the soul are. I encourage you to read the book to fully understand what they are, it helped me a lot to know and understand what these wounds were about, and they were part of my healing.

Lise says that the five wounds of the soul are: rejection, abandonment, humiliation, betrayal, and injustice.

According to Lise, the rejection wound was formed from conception to one year of age by the same-sex parent. The person with the rejection wound puts on the mask or the fleeing personality, which he will use to avoid suffering from the rejection wound. It can be easily noticed by the type of body the person with this wound has. Generally, he has a skinny body, almost pure skin and bone, as if wanting to disappear or not want anyone to notice him for fear of rejection. His back is hunched over with his shoulders forward and his hands attached to his body. Sometimes, his body is fragmented; the bottom part does not match the top part, and vice versa. They like solitude and prefer to be alone, constantly looking for the same-sex parent's love, and they can't believe someone can love them. Panic is the biggest fear of a person who suffers from rejection. Depending on how deep the wound is, the attitudes will be more accentuated, but the body will show you what your wound is. Sometimes you may think that you have another type of wound, but the body will always reveal and show your true wound; the body does not lie.

The rejection wound was created in the mother's womb when the mother, for some reason, rejected the baby. For example, when a woman suddenly becomes pregnant without being prepared, it makes the woman feels an immediate rejection of her baby. I believe this gives way to the mother's adverse symptoms during her pregnancy. She will have nausea and vomiting; this is what happened to me in my pregnancies. I love my children, and they are my world, but the moment I found out I was pregnant, I thought it was not the right time to have them. I can perfectly understand this wound because I also suffer from it.

This wound is deep since the person feels rejected inside, and their right to exist will always be questioned. This is one of my wounds. Before I began my healing, I lived with the thought, "I didn't want to exist. I would have preferred not to exist because I came into this world only to suffer." Until I found this and other information, I realized that unconsciously, thinking that way, I was being ungrateful to God and for the life he had given me. After I realized this, I changed my way of thinking. Once again, I reiterate being aware of what you are doing wrong will lead you to heal yourself. Later, I will explain what exercises and programs I did that helped me heal. The person with the rejection wound prefers not to become attached to material things because they can run away without any problem when necessary.

This wound leads you to be a perfectionist. That is not good because you put many burdens on yourself by wanting everything to be perfect, and you also put burdens on others by expecting perfection from them. It is very stressful to live wanting to do everything perfectly. I was a perfectionist, and I even said it. I didn't realize that I wasn't doing myself a favor by setting high expectations that are often difficult to meet. The people around you will also suffer because perhaps they want to please you, but they live stressed, thinking that they will do things wrong and you will get upset. It's not healthy to live with this trait of the rejection wound.

I always thought I had a memory problem; I thought I had memory loss or short-term memory. I was talking to someone and would turn around and needed to remember what I was saying. I also have no memory of many parts of my life, the majority of them. I only remember a few things, the most significant. Now I know why; in her book, Lise explains that the fear of feeling panic causes memory loss.

The rejection wound will also make you feel twice the sadness that being rejected causes you. I felt a dagger buried in my heart whenever I received a rejection. But people who don't have this wound can't understand this feeling. You may think I am exaggerating, but I will give you an example of how it feels. The case of 29-year-old Bailey, who goes to buy alcohol at the liquor store but forgets her ID, has an argument with the storekeeper, and he doesn't sell her alcohol. When she leaves, she begins to cry profusely. You may think, "How can a grown woman cry for that reason?" Well, in reality, her wounds of rejection and humiliation hurt her to the core. In the face of any situation that makes them come out, they will manifest themselves in her inner child; that's why her frustration and cry. The bad part about this is that the deeper your rejection wound, the more it will manifest itself in people and situations, so you are rejected, or you rejected others. Until you manage to overcome it.

The second wound is the abandonment wound. This wound is developed when we are children. The mask that the person with this wound puts on is that of the dependent. Abandonment is when someone abandons us or leaves, and we don't see them anymore. Still, it can be any situation that is related to abandonment. For example, when your parents have to go out for whatever reason and they leave you in another person's care. The child may think they do not want him, which is why his parents didn't take him, and he feels abandoned. Anyone who has lost a parent in death carries the wound of abandonment. This wound causes the child to grow up with co-dependency or dependency. Dependence leads the person to think that they can't do anything on their own and need help to do whatever they need because they want to feel supported.

According to Lise, the abandonment wound is experienced with the parent of the opposite sex and with the same-sex parent. This wound can be noticed on the person's body because he is thin and stooped, lacking muscle mass. The arms are too long and close to the body. The person has big sad eyes. He likes attention because he wants to feel important. He does not want to be alone for some reason; he would rather be victimized by others than be alone. An example of this can be a single woman who can't find a partner to marry and marries anyone to not be alone. Or the classic example of the wife of an alcoholic who will not leave him even if he beats her. Because she prefers to be with that person than be alone, the person becomes blind to such a situation and prefers to excuse the man and believe that everything is going well. Simply because she is afraid of abandonment because she is a dependent person. She would rather be mistreated than be alone. The person with the abandonment wound feels sad when they are not invited to an event. They think they are not important, and that's why they don't get invited.

This person likes to play the victim to receive pity from others. He tends to create all kinds of problems for himself, especially about his health, because he wants to get the attention of others, and he needs to feel supported. He always asks for the opinion of others. He could be perceived as lazy. But in reality, they don't like to do activities alone because they need the presence of others to feel supported. They will use blackmail or manipulation to get what they want.

I can give you an example of what the abandonment wound feels like. I suffered from neglect as a child. But first, let me tell you how I got to this point. As a family on my father's side, our outstanding trait or wound is injustice, so I feel very inclined to do something when I see injustice. But I try to restrain myself because the truth is that you can never win; in this world, there is no justice. When I was eight years old, my biological father was killed; he was my adoptive mother's brother. He was helping fight for a cause and was one of the leaders.

After winning the cause, he was killed; my mom says that someone tried to get her into a car against her will after that happened, and she thought someone was sent to harm her. So we had to flee from where we lived, in the beautiful port of Acapulco, to live in a town an hour away. Once there, my adoptive father decided to go to work in the United States. After a year, my mom divorces him. My mom had depression for a while and then found a job where she had to travel. And then, my sister had to move to another city to study; I was left alone in the "care" of my grandfather, who didn't look after me. I was alone most of the time and used to go to my friend's houses to play; sometimes, they would invite me to eat with them. I remember when my mother used to return from her trips and left, I always felt devastated and hopeless. Because I knew I wouldn't have anyone to take care of me.

That happened to me as a child when I faced that situation, and it continued to happen to me as an adult, but I wasn't aware of it. But I remember when my mom was visiting me around the year 2017. The day she left, I felt really bad, with that same hopelessness I felt when I was a child when my mom would leave. It was my abandonment wound. Although I was an adult, I never questioned that feeling. Even after I had been to therapy and seen psychologists, they never really helped me. Therefore it is crucial to find a psychologist who wants to help you because some just do it for the money. Due to the above, I was a co-dependent or dependent person, and I have worked a lot on that. There can be many kinds of dependency, such as on people, things, work, or helping others. I think I had most of them, but the most notable and profound were the co-dependency on my work and my desire to help others. I would prefer to work more and thus not realize my problems, and if someone told me about their problems, I would stay awake at night thinking about how I could help that person. I used to go out of my way to help others, putting my interests aside. Some people can't understand this and may say, "how dumb," but you do this due to your wound. You become an "empathic" person and give until it hurts. But now I have changed my thinking, and I know that the first person I have to help is me.

I still like to help others, but my family and I come first; I will if I can help someone else, I will. I learned to be a little selfish but healthy selfishness, to take care of myself first; there is nothing wrong with that.

The feeling that abandonment trauma leaves you is hard to understand. You will only understand it when you have experienced it yourself. When you live with the trauma of abandonment by your parents, you will live with a feeling of hopelessness all your life. Because living knowing that the people, who should have taken care of you and watched over you, rejected you will mark your life forever. This is my case; as I said before, my parents didn't want me; and they gave me away.

The abandonment trauma will lead you to believe that you are inadequate, that no one can love you, and you are not special to anyone. Why? Because you didn't receive love, nor did anyone foster in you that you were someone dear and special. You will never say it out loud, but in your subconscious mind, there will always be "I'm not enough," "I'm not worth it," "I don't deserve," and things like that. You will feel the same if you had your parents, but they never showed you affection or attention as a child because they were absent parents.

Let's look now at the humiliation wound created, according to Lise, through our physical functions of the body, such as speaking, listening, etc. This wound is created by being humiliated or embarrassed by one of your parents. The body of the person with this wound is round, robust, and has a round face. He protects himself with the masochist's mask. He feels humiliated and is afraid of being humiliated. The masochist will do anything for others. He doesn't feel worthy of deserving something, and he feels worthless and ashamed of himself, which is why he also has a body that embarrasses him. How often have we not seen someone with clothes that do not look good on them? And one says how come he dresses like that? He does it so that others see him badly, and thus he continues to humiliate himself. His wound is very deep if he wears small clothes revealing excess fat.

The masochist doesn't like to be controlled; he wants others to see that he does not give up or is firm in his decisions. For this reason, he will carry more emotional loads, and his body will show it, he has a wider back to carry more weight.

The person with the humiliation wound is usually a charismatic person who likes to tell jokes and be funny because it is a way of humiliating himself. You will know them as the "class clowns." No one will notice that behind that mask is a person who feels ashamed. Of course, depending on how deep his wound is, the more he will show all those characteristics. If his wound is not that deep, he may only show some characteristics.

Now let's talk about the betrayal wound. You can betray, or someone can betray you. This wound is developed as a child between the ages of two and four and is lived with the parent of the opposite sex. The mask the person will wear will be that of the controller but is a different type of control from that of the masochist.

He needs to be the center of attention of his mother or father of the opposite sex. This wound can be noticed by the person's body type. In men, the upper part is very muscular, and in women, in the lower part, the hips are wide. They tend to be strong and responsible people. They want to control everything so that everything goes well. If things don't go the way they want, they get upset and angry without letting others know.

He always tends to think ahead, anticipate and control everything to prevent a betrayal. He doesn't like being late because otherwise, he won't be in control of things. If you put something where it shouldn't go, the controlling person will be angry if you don't fix it. That was my case; I didn't like it when someone moved things from where I thought they should be. Now I realize it was a heavy burden for me, and I also imposed that burden on others since they feared that I would be upset if things didn't turn out the way I wanted them. Now, I don't care if something is five centimeters to the left or right of where I put them or wanted them to be. I prefer to live in peace.

The masochist finds it difficult to let other people do something he usually does. Because he thinks they won't do it the way he would. It is difficult for him to delegate and trust others. He believes that he is the only one who will do things well. That is a limiting belief, for sure. He says to himself, "if I don't do things, they don't go well." He wants to control other people's lives by telling them what to do. But they can't tell him what to do; he hates it. They think they have the absolute truth and want to impose their beliefs on others. He always wants to be right. He is very interested in his reputation; he would rather lie as long as his reputation is intact. He changes temperament from one minute to another.

The person with the betrayal wound does everything to be responsible, strong, and important because he does not want to be betrayed by someone or betray someone. They find it challenging to deal with people who take a long time to explain something; they will interrupt before they finish speaking.

If he gets sick, he tries to recover fast to continue his normal life, but if someone with whom he has commitments gets sick, he will be upset. I have traits of this wound in me; I'm a responsible person, and I don't like getting sick, so I continue working. But now I try not to be like that; I try to be balanced, and I don't want to go to extremes. I lead a more relaxed life in terms of that, and my body has changed. I don't have the masochist body anymore.

Let's move on to the fifth wound, the wound of injustice. This wound developed with the parent of the same sex between the ages of four and six. The person with this wound wears the mask of rigidity to protect himself. His body is very thin, rigid, and as perfect as possible. He is a perfectionist and an inflexible person. He crosses his arms very often. When he makes decisions, he doubts a lot about his decisions. He doesn't like to be late, but he is always late because it takes him a long time to get ready. He likes to give orders and demands a lot of himself. He doesn't like receiving gifts because he feels obligated to return the favor.

I can identify with this wound in some aspects; I was a perfectionist and even said it with pride. The person with this wound doesn't feel appreciated or valued. According to him, nobody treats him as he deserves. You will identify the rigid by the color of the clothes he wears. He always wears black or dark clothes because he doesn't want to feel. He may be a little envious because he envies those who have more than him and thinks they don't deserve it. He feels he is just and always wants everything to be that way. The person with this wound needs to prove to the world that they are worth it, the best, do things very well, can do everything better, and the list goes on. The truth is that to do this is tiring; that's how I felt. I felt the need to prove to the world that I'm worth it, but the reality is that we don't have to prove anything to anyone. We don't need to prove that we can or that we are capable, but the injustice wound unconsciously leads us to do this. This wound leads people to act as if they were righteous, I have seen people behave this way, but the truth is that the only just person is God. We see people with this wound commenting on social networks about what is fair or unfair to them; they can't help it and must leave their comments. You must be careful if you have this wound because injustice will continue to appear until you overcome it. This person will always be in a state of flight and fight, always doubting others, thinking that someone wants to hurt him or there is a possibility that someone will hurt him. He lives in fear that something will happen to him when in reality, he is safe; there is no reason why he should feel threatened. I think it's because the person is so afraid of injustice that he tries to keep himself safe.

But the sad reality of the human race is that there are injustices everywhere, and they can happen anytime. We live in a world plagued by them.

If you have identified yourself with some of the traits in each of these wounds, be aware that the more traits you have, the deeper your wound is. Lisc gives a more detailed description of each wound in her book.

If you are now thinking, "none of those situations concern me because my childhood was beautiful and my family was not perfect, but we were happy." Then keep reading because perhaps you will realize it wasn't like that. Most people have grown up in dysfunctional families; therefore, we have been psychologically affected. Examples of dysfunctional families are a family where the parent left home or perhaps passed away and is now a single-parent family. A family with a parent with a personality disorder, either a psychopath or narcissist. A family where one of the parents is an alcoholic or is addicted to gambling. A family where there is domestic violence, and a family where the father and the mother are present, but they are absent parents. They are not there emotionally, and they neglect their children. Unfortunately, the latter was the case with my children. I was an absent mother, but I wrote a letter apologizing to them once I realized it.

Maybe now you are thinking, "well, yes, in my family, there were some things that happened, but it wasn't that bad." What happens is that we have a selective memory. We only want to remember good memories, not bad ones, and block them from our memory. Also, the first defense mechanism of the human being is denial. So if someone tells us that a person we love did something bad to us or did something bad, the first thing we will say is, "I don't think that person did that." With that thinking, we protect ourselves from the sadness and disappointment we would feel if we knew that person was not who we thought he was. Especially if it's a family member. In the memories of our immediate family, we only want to remember good memories. We block bad memories from our minds to protect ourselves from what can hurt us. For this reason, even if we had thousands of bad memories, we instead focus on just that one beautiful memory of our family.

For example, if your father was a drunk and mistreated your mother. All you remember is when he took you and your family to the beach and had a great time. So in your mind, your father was not bad, nor was your childhood bad. Our brain clings to that one happy memory, there could be thousands of bad memories, but our brain only wants to remember the happy memory.

I recommend reading the book "The Five Wounds" to fully understand what they are about. If you identify yourself with any of these wounds, I will explain later what I did and what you can do to heal from them. Now, let's take a closer look at what narcissism is and how it affects people.

CHAPTER 5
NARCISSISM IN MY LIFE

As I said earlier, I consider Narcissism a silent pandemic that many still don't know about and need to know what it is. I will dedicate several chapters to discuss this because I think people must know about it.

Before, when I used to hear that word, it made me laugh because I thought, "that person looks at himself a lot in the mirror because he thinks he's handsome." But what is narcissism? And to what extent can living with a narcissistic person affect you?

Now I realize that I grew up surrounded by narcissistic people. My father had narcissistic traits, but I don't blame him because my grandfather was a narcissist, and I'm sure he was affected by him. These behaviors are passed on from one generation to the next until someone wakes up and breaks that chain of destruction. Some of their descendants can become narcissists, or the opposite may happen; they can become empathetic people, which was my case. I leave the description of empathy and what an "empath" person is in the index.

Narcissism is a common personality disorder, believe it or not. A narcissistic person can cause a lot of suffering to other people. Many people suffer psychologically from living with these types of people, and it takes years to recover from their trauma. Dr. Christane Northrup says others suffer damage to their health. For example, they suffer from autoimmune diseases like adrenal fatigue, IBS, or irritable bowel syndrome. They can't lose weight, are always tired, and go to the doctor, and the doctor can't treat them. What happens is that when you live with a narcissist, you are always on edge and live under constant stress. As a result, your cortisol levels are always high, causing the disease yourself. But what is narcissism? You can go back to page 24 to see the description, but here is more information about it.

Here are some traits of a narcissist:
-He believes he is superior to everyone (Grandiose thinking)
-Egocentric
-Wants to be treated differently from others
-He feels like he is special
-He throws a tantrum when you don't do what he says
-They are attractive and charming people
-They are competitive (they are the only ones with the best achievements)
-They don't listen to others (they have the absolute truth)

A true narcissist will never identify himself with these traits. He will never accept that he is a narcissist. If you live with one, don't tell him he is a narcissist, you risk being subjected to verbal or physical aggression from him. Instead, learn what that is and the tactics they use to manipulate others. There are covert narcissists and integrated narcissists; the integrated ones and the psychopaths are the worse. You can learn more about this on the YouTube channel Noche de Psicoterapia (Psychotherapy Night) from Peruvian Psychologist Fernando Leiva (English subtitles).

You may wonder how a narcissistic person can affect another person. They can't be that bad, right? But a narcissistic person is selfish, and others must be there to please him. He is like a black hole; it sucks everything in its path, he can only receive but can never give, and in this way, he affects the lives of the people who live with him or her.

Something I can share with you from my experience living with a family with narcissistic traits is that they are always calling others derogatory names like "that fat one," "that skinny one," "that ugly one," and so on. That is normal behavior in a family of that type. Also, calling yourself names like "I'm dumb" and "I'm stupid" and feeling superior to others for a particular reason you justify, like your family is superior to others. This is something inside you and is emphasized as you grow up. You are special because your family is of a superior race; you are from a particular place, etc., for whatever reason.

But it doesn't mean my family is bad; on the contrary, empathy characterizes my family. We are known for it, and my family is much appreciated.

Unfortunately, when a person is affected by a narcissist, then that person will go on to marry a narcissist; like a moth to the flame, it's something you can't avoid. Many people call that chemistry, but it's how you were programmed. Most likely, you share a wound with that person that's why you feel attracted to him. The narcissist's attitudes attract you because you are familiar with them; you have seen them in someone else. For this reason, many wonder why their love life sucks. It's because they keep attracting people with this personality disorder. The only way they can avoid this is to learn what a narcissist is and be aware of his tactics.

But how does the abuse of a narcissistic father or mother affect their children? Let's look at this in the next chapter.

CHAPTER 6
NARCISSISTIC ABUSE FROM PARENTS TO THEIR CHILDREN

How does the abuse of narcissistic parents affect their children? Let's look at some subtle ways narcissistic parents abuse their children. You don't need to raise your hand to harm them. Psychological abuse exists when someone is being manipulated, such as by playing with the feelings and emotions of the child. The father could be a sadistic person. He wants to be the most important person in the family and demands all the attention for himself. The father or mother wants to be the only one in charge, leaving aside what the other parent says, depending on who the narcissist is. What the other says doesn't matter, leading to an imbalance of powers and creating confusion in the children.

I will give you an example: The mother gives her children chores to do at home, the father comes and gives his children a new task, and the mother tries to explain she has already told them what to do and, as a good dictator, the father will not even consider what the mother has said, thus weakening the mother's authority over the children. The mother can't do anything about it and will be disarmed by not knowing what is happening. She knows something is wrong with what just happened, but she doesn't know what it is; she will relive the same scene many times and only remain silent and sad that this happened. She will think it's male chauvinism, but in reality, it's about the father's manipulation to have the children and her subjugated. The children will learn that only he is in charge, and just like the mother, they don't want to upset him. They will do everything possible so he is always happy, and they will do whatever he asks, so he doesn't get angry. The mother is so afraid of contradicting him, and the children perceive it, so they act accordingly. They are not aware that there is something wrong with this situation. A person must not change just because they want to please others.

The narcissistic father always wants to be the center of attention in the family. If someone else wants to take that place from him, they will be mistreated by him. The children will compete to be the father's favorite child. He has created this competitive environment in the family. Children always find themselves doing and acting in ways the narcissist likes by changing their personality to be accepted by him. They will carry this type of behavior into their adulthood by trying to please others, changing their character, to make others like them.

When the narcissistic father wants something from his wife or children, he will use love bombing to get it. He will treat them affectionately and say nice things to them to get what he wants. Once he gets it, he will continue humiliating and mistreating them. And this happens all the time, but the victims will always fall for it because they need love and affection, and he knows it very well.

The narcissist was trapped between the ages of three and five, and when a child of that age is not given what he wants, he throws a tantrum. The same happens with the narcissist; when someone in the family doesn't do what he says or ruins his plans, he will try to get revenge. The family constantly fears doing something the narcissist doesn't like because they already know he will try to avenge. No one will talk about these things happening within the family because they don't realize what is going on, the manipulation in which they live. As I said before, this is a silent pandemic. And if someone tells what is happening, it will only bring mockery from others; they will say they imagine things. And if you tell someone within the family, you will only get denial; they will deny that this is going on. As human beings, we refuse to think that there are bad people in this world, especially within our families. Our first reaction to these types of situations is to say, "you are crazy," "it's not true," and "you are exaggerating." Thus denying the reality of the person who has already realized something is wrong with the family. Everyone knows something terrible is happening, but no one will tell the other.

For the narcissist, there are only his needs, so he will buy everything he wants for himself, even if it's costly. If someone else in the family needs something, the narcissist will say it's expensive. His free time will be spent on whatever he wants to do and not spending time with his family or what they want to do. The family will always live in the background, accepting the crumbs and whatever the narcissist wants to give them. The mother will only live in anguish for her children, she knows that this behavior on the father's part is wrong, but she can't say anything. If she complains, he will mistreat her, justify himself, and explain why he can't give his children certain things. He will even turn the children against their mother.

I make a parenthesis here to explain that the narcissist's immediate family, his wife, and children, will always be in the background, and his parents and siblings will always be his main family. You might know men who are like that, and this is due to the traumatic bond. I'll explain a traumatic bond later, but we are not talking about a healthy family bond; we are talking about an unhealthy one. God says, "a man will leave his father and mother to become one flesh with his wife." But the narcissist doesn't see it that way because his family, his mother, and siblings are the ones who experienced the trauma or abuse of the narcissistic father with him. Therefore, they are his main family, and his wife and children are always in second place. That's where the trauma bond comes in; everyone in his family developed a traumatic bond when the narcissist mistreated them. And because of that traumatic feeling, now everyone is united by it. According to the narcissist, "No one else can understand that feeling, only them."

Going back to the topic, the children will always want to be in good standing with the father, and that's why they will always side with him; this leaves the mother disarmed. There's nothing she can do about it; she'll keep quiet like always. First, she hasn't realized the manipulation she is experiencing; second, no one will believe her if she says something. If someone shares something like this with you, just listen, try to understand, and encourage them to seek professional help. You don't know if the person is being emotionally abused.

The narcissist humiliates and mistreats his victim, and she will be ashamed to talk about it with others, and he knows it. He knows she will not say what's going on within the relationship. She will suffer all that emotional abuse in silence. No one will notice, not even her children, because she won't tell them anything due to her love for them so they don't suffer. Unfortunately, children are affected by this, and there is nothing a person can do about it. Dr. Ramani Duvursula, an expert in Narcissism, says, "If the mother stays with the narcissist, the damage is greater, and if she leaves him, the damage will be less, but they will still be damaged."

Notably, he is a narcissist because he was also affected by a narcissist that marked him forever. He will carry his traumas with him into his adult life and relive them in his home. Of course, not all children will repeat these behaviors; some will learn from the bad experience and will not want to repeat it. The only remedy is to "wake up" and seek professional help to heal from these traumas and live a "normal" life. If you know someone with narcissistic traits, don't tell him he is a narcissist; just encourage him to seek professional help.

Unfortunately, this is happening in many homes at this very moment. And the family doesn't even realize what they are experiencing. They think it is normal. That's why I wrote this book to help those people. I hope to reach most of them.

But what happens in a relationship with a narcissistic partner? Let's see this in the next chapter.

CHAPTER 7
NARCISSISTIC RELATIONSHIP

The narcissistic relationship goes through several stages. In the end, the person will not even realize when the narcissist caught her, used her, and discarded her. Usually, the stages of a narcissistic relationship are: the choosing of the victim, falling in love, isolation, control, and abandonment or discarding.

The narcissist, male or female, is an attractive and charming person who always attracts the attention of others. He is usually a *Don Juan*, and when he chooses someone, that person feels like the "chosen" one. He selected her among all the other women; she is privileged. Everything she likes, he likes; as she is, he will be. He does all this to deceive her into thinking they are soul mates. He's going to use love bombing, he's going to bombard her with love, and that is how he will wrap it up. He will do things for her out of the ordinary, so he will lure her in faster. For example, he will arrive at her house without warning with a hundred red roses, at her work with a surprise, and do everything he can to be near her all the time. And she will think he is doing it because he loves her. When you just meet someone, and they do this kind of thing, be careful; it may be a sign that he is a narcissist. The person will feel like they are in a fairy tale because they will think they have found their prince charming. But that's not true; it's just a facade. But surprise! She has already fallen into the claws of the narcissist, and what other people say about him will not matter. She will fight to be with her prince charming until death. This way, she will begin to distance herself from her family and friends, which is what the narcissist wants because he will do whatever he wants with her. He wants to be the only person in her life. Although her relatives try to warn her about him being a bad person, she will not believe it. She will think, "he loves me, and that's why he is with me, and he would never hurt me because he loves me; he has shown it to me." Since her family and friends had warned her about him, and she ignored them when the narcissist begins mistreating her she can't call them to share with them what is happening.

Thus the narcissist will begin with his deceit, psychological abuse, and humiliation. The narcissist likes to use the triangulation with his victim, which consists of putting a third person in discord in the relationship. He will look at other women with lust in front of his partner. He's going to say things like, "oh, look how pretty that woman is," or when he goes out, he's going to say, "I'm going to see my girlfriends," which will make her jealous. It will also make her feel insecure. Since he is a sadist, he likes to say such things to leave the person thinking about him and wondering if it's true; he loves that. He constantly seeks attention; he wants her to think of him all the time. He will use guilt to manipulate her. He will always play the victim, using his past to get her to pity him. Remember that the narcissist had an unhappy childhood. He will use that pity to make her do things he wants her to because she will say, "poor man, he suffered a lot."

Usually, the most predominant prey of the narcissist is dependents and histrionics, opting more for the dependent since they are empathetic people. An empathetic person will always put other people's needs before their own. And the narcissist only knows how to receive, not give. He will use his children if they have them and say, "do it for them," or perhaps he will use her parents and say, "what are your parents going to say." You can recognize he is a narcissist because of his lies. He is a habitual liar, always lying. If he doesn't lie, he uses gaslighting to lure his victim. Gaslighting means that, although what they say is a lie, they will make the person believe it's true. For example, he will say he said something when he didn't. But he will say he said it so many times that the other person will doubt the truth. He even makes the other person feel crazy because they don't remember.

Despite the psychological abuse she is experiencing, she will always excuse him. Because the "poor man was mistreated as a child, poor him" or for any other excuse she makes. Only her friends and family watching the abuse will realize she is being abused, but she can't see it as if she is under a spell. The relatives of these women always tell them, "how dumb are you? Why are you still with that man?"

She cannot believe that a person, who showed her so much love at the beginning and even gave her life for her, is the bad person everyone says. Remember that denial is the brain's first defense mechanism to not feel pain. She will continue to deny what her relatives say is true.

Single moms should be cautious with narcissistic men in this regard. Those whom many of us call "Don Juan" or "womanizers" because this type of narcissist wants to find his mother's love in his partner. For this reason, at the beginning of the relationship, he will fight to be with her with his cloak and sword, which she will confuse with true love.

Why is he looking for a single mother? Because she is a mother, he looks at her as his mother. From the beginning, he knows he will receive a mother's affection from her that he didn't receive from his mother. But when he realizes she is not his mother, he leaves her and humiliates her while leaving. He will humiliate her by looking at other women lewdly because he can only look at other women like that. He can't look at her like that because she is "his mother." If she tries to leave him, he will blackmail her, so she doesn't leave him; he will tell her that he will kill himself if she leaves, which makes her think he loves her, but that is not true; he only loves himself. He does that because he wants to leave her first. That's why we see many women with children from different fathers because the man comes looking for his mother's affection. Since he can't find it, he leaves her for another woman. He can't find that mother's love he didn't receive. Some women, too, look for their father's affection in their husbands, and they look at them as their fathers. But there is hope for these people; they can change their personalities with professional help and humility. Although it is said that a narcissist will never change.

Returning to the topic, narcissists also use the silent treatment to blackmail their victims into getting what they want. They stop talking to them for days or weeks when they get upset. The integrated narcissist will even make her quit her job and depend on him; thus, he will control her, and she won't leave him.

In the discard stage, he will abandon her for another woman; it's most likely that he already had her before leaving her. Now, she feels devastated, thinking he left because of something she did, and she blames herself. The narcissist is not empathetic; he doesn't care at all how she feels or what she is going through. But he'll always have her on his contact list just in case he needs her again. He knows that when he calls her, she will take him back.

But his lack of empathy in the discard stage is not the worst part; the worst part is that he will discredit her with her family and friends. It's called a "smear campaign." He will say bad things about her, and when she denies it, no one will believe her because he always showed himself as a good and loving man. She never said anything about what was going on in the relationship, so this will make her relatives not believe her when she tells them the truth.

The victim may never realize what happened to her and will long for the narcissist to return. Or on the other hand, she may understand what happened to her, the hell she lived through, and from there, the victim will try to find information that will help her heal her wounds.

After the narcissistic abuse, the person is destroyed; the psychological abuse was so much that they will no longer want to find another partner. But everything she lived through will help her mature, and she can only learn from what happened to her and move on. It may be that from there, she becomes an advocate of letting other people know about narcissistic people.

Many men and women may be in a narcissistic relationship and don't know, but how can they find out? Let's see this in the next chapter.

CHAPTER 8
AM I IN A NARCISSISTIC RELATIONSHIP?

Let's look at situations that will help you know if you are in a narcissistic relationship. Let's see how it feels to be in a narcissistic relationship. It feels like you are living a dream relationship with your prince charming, but at the same time, something is wrong, and you don't know what it is; you can't give it a name. You are confused; you think, "maybe it is my fault that things are not going right." The narcissist will always be making you feel bad with demeaning comments. Telling you, "you are stupid," "you can't live without me," "without me, you are nothing," and things like that. He mistreats you, but at the same time, he bombards you with love. He humiliates and mistreats you, but then he tells you "my life" and "my love," and you believe and forgive him.

Due to the emotional abuse, it's difficult for you to make decisions because you can't think straight. Even though you know it's a bad relationship, you will not do anything about it; you will put up with the abuse. You feel bad, but you will deny your truth. You might think you are exaggerating, that all this is normal in a relationship, and you are drowning in a glass of water. You will deny your reality in order not to damage the relationship. The narcissist uses gaslighting to manipulate you, which makes things worse. He tells you something, and then when you ask him why he told you that, he will deny that he said it, and you will doubt your sanity. You will constantly be sick and go to the doctor, who tells you that there is nothing wrong with you and "you are crazy," basically. But really, it's all a consequence of your narcissistic relationship. Dr. Christane Northrup, whom I mentioned earlier, calls narcissists energy vampires. She says that this type of relationship, whether with a family member or your partner, can lead to autoimmune diseases and mysterious illnesses that don't respond to any kind of medicine or diet. None of that can help because everything is caused by the energy vampire. Until you heal that part of your life energetically, you will be able to heal physically. She says that the stress caused by being in that relationship causes cellular inflammation, which is the root cause of all chronic degenerative diseases. The stress of wanting to change a person and dealing with their negativity releases stress hormones in your body. And under so much pressure, your adrenal glands produce cortisol in the body; when these remain high, the body produces these inflammatory chemicals called decline as cortisol. And when you're in a narcissistic relationship, it's like being on cortisone medication all the time. Its symptoms are headaches, joint pain, arthritis, fibromyalgia, digestive problems, lupus, weight gain, and eventually diabetes. That's why you have a terrible diet. You want to eat sweets all the time, like donuts and soda, because when you're under stress, you don't want to cook nutritious meals. Excess cortisol makes you want to eat sweets or alcohol.

A narcissistic relationship is one-sided; there will never be "you and me" but just "me." You will always be alone; unfortunately, you will never count on your partner. You're going to be doing things to make the relationship work; he's never going to do anything because he doesn't care, and you'll feel like a failure. The narcissist will always make you think you are not enough, which makes you feel ashamed of the relationship. You feel ashamed of living in a fake relationship, and others don't know.

You constantly argue for any reason, which is very exhausting; everything becomes a discussion, even the silliest things. That makes you not want to do anything, forget everything, and live in depression.

Besides, everything is a problem for the narcissist, even the most trivial things to do around the house. Like a little boy, he only wants to do what he enjoys and not what has to be done. For example, cleaning the house and buying groceries is a constant struggle; it's exhausting. Everything ends in arguments, and he always wants to win; you never win, and you have to give up; if not, it's a never-ending story. You prefer to stay quiet because you don't want to argue. You're going to let him do what he wants, go out and do things he likes, and you don't say anything as long as you don't have to argue with him. You think you will carry the relationship in peace by doing this, and he will see that and change, but it's not true. He will never change because the narcissist lacks empathy; and will never think about you and your needs. You will live in depression and anxiety because every day, he will be making your life impossible for any reason. All of this leads you to be another person, more withdrawn; you no longer like the things you liked and find no pleasure in them. If you like to party, now you don't because he makes it impossible for you to go to a party. You no longer want to go out with your friends because you are ashamed of your life. You don't want people to ask you, "and your husband?" And you can't tell them the truth about what's happening, that he only does what he wants and what you want to do doesn't matter to him. He will say you're just like him, but don't believe him; you can't be as bad as him. This is a tactic narcissist use called leveling.

If you identify any of these behaviors in your partner or family member, stay away from that person. What can help you is to practice "Love Zero" or "Family Zero," a concept by Dr. Iñaki Piñuel in his books of the same name that I recommend you read.

According to Dr. Piñuel, the traumatic bond reveals why victims return to their perpetrators repeatedly. He says that the victim will return an average of seven times. They will continue to be a victim of the abuser if the person doesn't work on their cognitive dissonance and trauma bond. But what is the trauma bond?

According to the online article in the Medical News Today, "What is the traumatic bond?" a traumatic bond is a connection between an abused person and the person who abuses them. It usually occurs when the abused person develops sympathy or affection for the abuser. In theory, trauma bonding can happen in any situation that involves one person abusing or exploiting another. This may include situations involving: domestic violence, child abuse, incest, kidnapping cases, human trafficking, religious extremism, or cults, among others. The main sign that a person has become attached to an abuser is trying to justify or defend the abuse. A person emotionally attached to the abuser might say, for example, "He's only like that because he loves me so much, you wouldn't understand."

In other words, the victim developed a traumatic bond with her abuser, which is why she always returns to him. If you have identified your relationship with a narcissistic relationship, get out of it as soon as possible. No, you are not crazy; you are experiencing emotional abuse; seek professional help. Go to your family and friends and tell them what is happening; maybe there is someone who can help you. But the first thing that will help you is to know and understand you are in a narcissistic relationship. After you become aware and learn what that is, learn the tactics the narcissist uses to manipulate you so he can no longer manipulate you. The best thing you can do is to get out of the relationship and leave that person. Don't have any contact with him. But if you can't leave, you can practice what Dr. Ramani recommends: "radical acceptance," accept your situation but don't get involved with the narcissist.

The same article says that breaking a traumatic bond can be challenging and takes time, but it's possible. It cites The National Domestic Violence Hotline, which suggests that people can do three things to break the traumatic bond. 1. Focus on the present. 2. Focus on the evidence, and 3. Practice positive self-talk.

In the next chapter, I will tell you everything I did to heal from my traumas, and I hope my experience helps you too.

CHAPTER 9
MY HEALING BEGINS

I wonder how a person can live tormented by their traumas without even being aware of them. Without knowing that something is affecting their lives and it's not normal, there is no one to tell them about it. Incredible but true. Before I realized what I'm telling you in the book, I was always sick, almost dying, had no energy, allergies, infections, and felt like an 80-year-old. And whenever I went to the doctor, they never found anything; there was nothing wrong with me; basically, I was "crazy." Hence, I decided to look for unconventional healing to alleviate my discomfort. I started healing myself with natural medicine and vitamins, eating healthier, and exercising.

One of my symptoms was depression, which is very common these days, but it's not the root of the problem, but the effect of the cause, because everything in life is cause and effect. If you really want to heal, you must look for the cause of your depression to start your recovery. Depression is a clinical illness that must be treated. It's normal to feel sad for a while, but when it affects your daily life, you should seek professional help.

I suffered from depression for many years, but in my case, being aware of what was causing the illness cured me. As I said at the beginning, I'm not a psychologist; I can only share with you what happened to me. In 2017, I did a clinical study of a new depression medication. But they don't tell you if you're taking the actual drug or it's a placebo. The study lasted the whole year, and I had to answer questions about how I felt every month. Answering them made me aware that I didn't have depression and my problem came from another source; it was a person causing the illness. When I realized it, it completely disappeared. Incredible but true. And to this day, I no longer take medication for depression.

If you suffer from depression, I recommend seeing a professional who can help you through techniques such as the "golden thread." This technique can help you find where your negative thoughts come from, thoughts of uselessness or not wanting to live, which are some of the things that go through your mind when you have depression.

We already talked about traumas and their definitions. Now how can a person overcome their traumas? Being aware that you have one is a good start; it leads you to know you have a problem and to seek help; the humility to do this is essential. What helped me was learning what my traumas were, and realizing that I had a problem helped me focus on it and seek the specific information I needed. When you read the information, it's like something clicks in your brain. You can understand exactly what is happening to you and why you behave in specific ways or do things in a certain way; that helps you greatly.

It also helps you to learn that you are not the only one, the first, or the last in this life that has traumas. And unfortunately, this will continue to happen to other people; it will take away that psychological weight you have been carrying and have not realized. Being aware of the things that happened to you and accepting them will help you tremendously to assimilate them. Knowing that many of them were not your fault will help to move on with your life. It's also vital that you get professional help.

Surely by reading this book, you have realized some things you can work on. If you have recognized you have a problem, you are already on your way to your healing.

Another one of my problems was post-traumatic stress. You develop PTSD after you have experienced traumatic events; it can be something that happened to you only once or repetitive events such as emotional abuse. And this impacts your emotions, feelings, short-term memory, and intentional capacity in numerous capacities and cognitive competencies. Dr. Piñuel says that perhaps a person confuses post-traumatic stress with Alzheimer's, an organic syndrome, or a brain tumor because it makes you forget things or can't concentrate. That was my case; I thought one of those was my problem.

There were days when I felt terrible to the point of not wanting to live, and I didn't know why, but it was rare; it happened to me every six months or so, but it increased during the quarantine. I was very active in all aspects of my life. I think it was a way of forgetting about what I was experiencing without realizing it. When the pandemic started, I was devastated because I could no longer do what was helping me cope with my situation. I felt sad and hopeless. During the episodes, I would wake up and feel like I couldn't take it anymore, and I didn't want to live anymore or wanted to "cease to exist," as I called it.

I think it was the lowest point in my life. I'm glad that God helped me and used my friends to help me to cope with the situation. One of them was my friend and therapist Nicky Nava who lives nearby; she was always there to listen to me. That year I finally understood why this was happening to me with the explanation given by Dr. Piñuel. He says that the brain is undergoing a process of high stress and emotional abuse by a perpetrator or psychopath, such as hostility, contempt, and denigration. This causes the victim to enter into confusion that begins to give way to post-traumatic damage. Victims have "burned their wiring" in their brains, so to speak. The brain has not been able to deal with that traumatic experience. This post-traumatic stress occurs equally in victims of a single event, such as rape, or several events, such as emotional abuse.

He says the person under the effect of post-traumatic stress wakes up one day and realizes she can't take it anymore. That her body doesn't obey her, that her mind is confused, that she can't handle life, that her emotions don't obey her or don't obey the control of reason. A disconnection occurs in the upper part of the brain, called the cerebral cortex, and the deeper areas of the interior part of the brain, which is the limbic system, the parts of the brain that regulate emotions, have been melted down with a malfunction.

The person who has experienced this so often can't identify that something different has happened in their brain and attributes it to their illnesses or depression. After learning all this, it doesn't happen to me anymore. I have taken control of my life and don't let anyone manipulate me by making me feel guilty, remorseful, or anything like that. I don't let anything external affect me. I have accepted that I cannot change people or situations; I can only change myself and how I see things.

One of the first tools I used to heal myself in 2020 was Tom Nuyen's Alive Academy course. He taught me how to get rid of all the defense layers I had put on myself since I was a child to protect myself from pain, harden my heart and not feel. By doing the course, I learned to love myself. Since I didn't know how to love myself. We just do things in life instinctively, like little animals, doing what we must, but we don't realize what it means to love ourselves and the most important things in life.

That day I felt self-love; I cried a lot. I was finally showing my inner self by allowing myself to feel without fear of anyone judging me. I'm a human who feels, laughs, and cries when necessary. Now I give myself the right to feel any emotion whenever I feel it. I love that course, and I recommend it to everyone. Through videos and exercises, it helps you to return to your natural state, like when you were a child when you weren't embarrassed or felt shame to show your feelings. It also enables you to shape your personality like a diamond and be different.

The first thing I did while doing this course was to buy myself a Barbie doll. I had always wanted to have one because I didn't have one as a child, and I lived with that sad emotion of not having one. So to get rid of that emotion, I decided to buy it myself. I purchased a beautiful 50th-edition Barbie doll. Of course, it's not to play with it; just knowing that I have it frees me from that feeling of being a "victim."

It should be noted that for some odd reason, I was finding all the information as I needed it, not before. In the year 2021, I decided to do something about my insomnia. I decided to see a therapist who recommended reading the book Forgiving Yourself and Others by Dr. Carolle Jean-Murat. It helped me a lot. I didn't know we store emotions like shame and guilt in our bodies. That's when I realized I hadn't forgiven myself. Before reading the book, I would wake up every night at 3:30 am, and would be there thinking, "why did I allow this? Why did I do this? Why didn't I do this and that?" Reading the book, I realized that I had made mistakes like any other human being, and if I had done something wrong, it was because I didn't know better. I made decisions with my knowledge at the time, and it wasn't because I was a bad person. I did the exercises in the book, and one of them was to write down the things I was ashamed of. Doing the exercises was challenging for me. There were many things that I was ashamed of, and I was even ashamed of what I was ashamed of. It's not easy to admit it, but if you want to heal, it's better to be honest and get everything that hurts you out of your system.

What were some of the things I was ashamed of? I was ashamed of being adopted, having had my daughters at the age of 16, of having made wrong decisions, among other things. But now I'm no longer ashamed; adoption happens in this world all the time and will continue to happen; it's something that is out of our control and not our fault. Unfortunately, I didn't have a role model in my life, and I made bad decisions, but that's life in the world we live in, and I don't blame anyone; it just happened.

After my mom divorced my dad in the eighties, she also

decided to go to the United States to work. A year later, she brought my sister and me over. At that time, my mom stayed at the house where she worked the whole week, so I only saw her on the weekends. My sister worked, so I was on my own to do whatever I wanted. And with my desire to be a part of something or have a family, I started hanging out with the wrong people. I got into gangs, but thank God, even though I was in that environment, I never did drugs or steal; I think it was because of my fear of God, instilled by my grandmother.

The boys respected me and took care of me, I had a sense of belonging, and they were like my family. In that place, I met my boyfriend, and after a year, I got pregnant, giving birth at 16. I was ashamed of that. I know I could have taken another path, but unfortunately, these are things that we'll see happen in this world throughout our lives.

After two years, I decided to fix my life and marry my boyfriend. But one day at night, I woke up choking on cigarette smoke because he smoked. At that moment, I thought to myself, "what am I doing? I can't marry him. I can't marry a drunk" because he smoked and drank. And I decided to walk away from the relationship. But he used to tell me, "if you leave me, I'll kill you and kill myself." I was very young and afraid he would do something like that. He was very violent, but how often has that not happened before? I asked God to help me get away from him, and he helped me.

Back on topic, after reading the book and doing the exercises, my guilty conscience disappeared. I no longer ask myself those questions at night. Now I try to be the best person I can and help others who are going through the same thing I went through. If you live with guilt for something you did or didn't do, I advise you to buy the book or do the exercise so you can see for yourself that this can help you. Write down everything you are ashamed of on paper and then burn it. Forgive yourself, we are imperfect human beings, and we make mistakes.

Speaking of trapped emotions, I also found a technique called

Raynor's Massage to eliminate trauma or trapped emotions. I liked it so much that I'm now a Certified Massage Therapist in this technique.

Then I found the book Familia Zero that I recommend you read. It helped me to understand that I had been affected by a dysfunctional family. I realized I had experienced neglect in my life, and this is common. The book helped me understand what it was like to live in a "zero family" and to give a name to those things I couldn't understand, which is called trauma. Many times simply giving your discomfort a name will help you heal. Also, being aware of the trauma we experienced as children and the trauma that was inherited from our ancestors will help us. We learned those distortions from our ancestors, such as living always catastrophizing, meaning we always think the worst will happen in any situation. We inherited their fears, greed, scarcity, and things like that, but of course, we also inherited their talents.

Psychologist Aaron T. Beck the developer of "Cognitive Therapy," calls this behavior a cognitive distortion. Cognitive distortions are irrational ideas that lead a person to generate automatic negative thoughts about things or events. I think these distortions are the limiting beliefs our ancestors instilled in us. See if you identify some of them in your behaviors. The psychologist divides them into 17 cognitive distortions, which are:

1. Jumps to negative conclusions like "I'm not going to pass the exam" when he should be thinking, "I trust what I studied, and I'll do well on the exam."

2. Catastrophizing, is when we evaluate a situation with the worst possible result. Thinking, "maybe if I drive, I end up crashing or running over a person," when we should think, "I trust my abilities because if I don't practice, I won't have experience."

3. Comparison, when a person constantly compares himself unfavorably with others thinking, "he has better grades than me," when he should think, "if I study, I will have good grades, and I will have done the best I could."

4. All or nothing thinking, something is either white or black,

there is no in between, for example, thinking, "if this person rejects me, I will no longer go out with anyone else because no one likes me" when in reality the person should think "I will hope for the best and if not, I hope to meet someone else."

5. Disqualification of the positive, when someone disqualifies the positive traits of a person by saying something like "that person was successful, but it was only by luck" when in reality we should give them credit and say something like "he did it because he prepared, worked hard and he did it."

6. Emotional reasoning, is when we reason according to our emotions and say something like "I'm afraid to get on a plane; flying is very dangerous" when we should think, "nothing bad will happen; it's very safe to fly."

7. Construction of personal worth based on external opinions, when we value ourselves according to what others think, for example, saying something like "my boyfriend says I'm stupid, he's surely right" when in reality she should think "That's his opinion about me, I think I'm capable."

8. Fortune telling, according to the person, they can predict a negative result, an emotion, or a future event, and they believe those predictions to be true; for example, they say, "if I apply for a scholarship, they will not give it to me" when they should think "I have the same chances of getting it than everyone and I trust my qualifications to get it."

9. Labeling, is when a person labels themselves or another person with a negative connotation such as "I am the worst player in the world, I'm a fool," when they should think "I do very well, and if I practice, I can become an excellent player."

10. Magnification, is a tendency to exaggerate the negative of a trait or situation, event, or person, for example, thinking, "he's not going to like my gift; it's very simple," when he should think, "I gave him something that came from my heart, he will like it."

11. Mind reading, is when a person believes that another is thinking negatively of them without evidence of it, for example, "my dad thinks I'm useless, but he doesn't tell me" when he

should think, "my dad loves me, and he thinks I can do anything I set my mind to."

12. Minimization, is the process by which some events, traits, or circumstances are minimized or insignificant, such as thinking, "my boyfriend gave me only a rose; he doesn't love me," when she should think, "how nice, he remembered me, what a nice detail."

13. Overgeneralization is drawing conclusions based on a few experiences or applying them to a range of unrelated situations, such as thinking, "my food burned, I can never do anything right," when you should be thinking, "you learn from your mistakes, the next time it will be much better."

14. Perfectionism, is when a constant effort is made for an internal or external representation of perfection to be fulfilled without examining whether it's reasonable, often to avoid a subjective experience of failure such as thinking, "if I don't want to lose, it's better not to play" when he should think "if I keep playing one day I will win."

15. Personalization, is when a situation, event, or reaction of others is taken personally without supporting evidence. For example, someone may think, "Pepe and Manuel are laughing; surely they are laughing about me," when he should ignore it and think, "Pepe and Manuel are having fun – I just remembered that I have something to do; I'm leaving".

16. Mental filters, is the process of focusing only on a negative aspect, detail, or situation so that its importance is magnified by putting the entire situation in a negative context, such as thinking, "I'm the worst; I lost my eraser" when he should think "I'm going to buy another one and I'm going to "erase" that from my mind ha ha".

17. Statements with "should" are internal expectations or demands on personal or other abilities or skills, but without analyzing whether they are reasonable in the context in which they are said, for example, saying, "I should have realized that it was wrong to ask so many questions in the meeting" but rather

say "I liked the meeting and learned a lot."

If you identify with any of these behaviors, acknowledge = you have them and try to change them. Maybe someone in your family did this, and you learned it, and now you do the same.

But back on topic, many families out there are being psychologically abused and suffering. And don't even know what they are going through at the hands of narcissistic parents, spouses, and psychopaths. I hope I can reach them with this information.

Through Dr. Piñuel I found a therapy to overcome traumas called EMDR, a specific technique to treat traumas. Although not many psychologists know this technique or are certified to do it, some are, like, Dr. Piñuel. I will leave you his information in the references. I advise you to find a psychologist who specializes in this if you want to try this technique. In my case, I found a virtual EMDR page, which you can use at your discretion. It worked for me, but each person is different, of course. I think doing the virtual therapy helped me because I had already worked through many of my traumas and was more receptive and ready to do it. If you want to do it, I advise you to prepare yourself first. I leave the information where you can do the online therapy in the references.

Let me give you an example of the result of one of my therapy sessions. I worked on all the memories that came to my mind, and that saddened me. I was doing something in my daily life, and suddenly they came to my mind (I call them pictures). Still, before 2021 all those memories came to mind from time to time; one of them was that I see myself as a child in my room, alone, sitting there playing. I always wondered why that memory would come to mind. What does it mean? While doing the therapy and answering the questions about how that memory makes me feel, I realized that this memory meant a feeling of hopelessness and the neglect I had experienced. And I had lived with that emotion almost all my life.

The situation I found myself in at that time was my adoptive parents had divorced, and my mother worked outside the home. I was 8 or 9 years old and alone with my grandfather. I had no one to take care of me, feed me, wash my clothes, help me with homework, or anything like that. My grandfather was a bad man, and I don't judge him; I know he also went through bad experiences in his life. I slept with fear at night that my grandfather would hurt me. I would only eat once a day, which was at school, because my grandfather would give me money to buy lunch. When my mom returned from her trips, I was happy, but when she left, I felt hopeless; as I had already mentioned, I still had that feeling as an adult. One day I took pills to take my life, but it didn't work.

During EMDR therapy, you are shown positive thoughts you can think so you can change your negative thoughts. For example, if you think, "I don't deserve" or "I should have done something," instead, you can think, "I deserve" or "I did what I could." While doing the therapy, those positive things come to mind, and your brain helps you with that. In one of the sessions, I saw that memory again. That little girl sitting there with those feelings of sadness and hopelessness. But suddenly, I saw her, and she turned around, looked at me, and smiled. That's when I told her that we didn't need anyone else now, that I would love her and take care of her; tears of sadness and joy came to my eyes. Since then, that memory no longer comes to mind. And so I worked all the sad memories I had kept in my mind with the EMDR therapy.

Something that helped me a lot, apart from all the courses, books, and information I found, was that I already have a purpose in life. I know what the key to happiness is despite having problems. I only needed to understand how the human brain and our psychology worked. I know where happiness comes from. A human being's happiness can be summed up with what one of the wisest men said. King Solomon said in Ecclesiastes 12:13, "The conclusion of the matter, everything

having been heard, is: Fear the true God and keep his commandments, for this is the whole obligation of man." There you have it, ladies and gentlemen, something so simple but profound. We were put in this world to worship God; that was all we had to do, but because of our first parents, Adam and Eve, and their disobedience, we are now in the conditions we are in. But despite that, we can still be happy if we obey God; when we fulfill our purpose, what we were created for, which was to worship him, we achieve happiness. But the further away we are from our source, our creator, the unhappy we are.

Many people think that to obey God, they must carry the Bible with them all the time, but that is not true. When you know you shouldn't lie or steal, you just have to practice it; you don't need to have the Bible with you.

Happiness is a mental state of mind; I have experienced it many times, making a fire in my head a problem. Then I fixed the problem in my head, and nothing outside of me happened. How ironic! True happiness is not achieved with money because even millionaires are unhappy; some even commit suicide. Our happiness doesn't depend on others either but on ourselves. Many people say, "I want to find a partner that can make me happy," but how will you find a partner to make you happy if you are not happy with yourself? You can't put that burden on someone else. Learn to be happy with yourself first.

Although now I don't consider myself an expert on these issues, I have been able to wake up and be more conscious. I can tell when someone is acting in certain ways, I know how to deal with them, and their behaviors no longer affect me.

Finding the information about the five wounds of the soul has helped me a lot. Doing the healing meditations has also helped me to heal my emotional wounds. I recommend you look for them on YouTube, but you can also find them on my channel @awakendespertarbook. Regarding this means of healing, each person has to decide whether to believe or not believe. As I said, there are things I believe in and others I don't, but I use whatever helps me, and what I think doesn't help me, I discard.

For example, the healing meditation on abandonment made me aware that I resented my biological parents, which I didn't want to admit. I thought that since they had not been part of my life, they had nothing to do with me, and I was wrong. Through the wound-healing meditations, I forgave my parents, let them go, and accepted them as they are because they, too, had traumas, and that's why they acted the way they did. After doing the meditation, it was as if the weight I had been carrying for many years was lifted. I can say it very easily now, but it cost me many tears. Many times we don't want to admit that we have resentment towards our parents, we think it is sacrilege, but that doesn't help us to heal; on the contrary. What we can do instead is identify the emotion, recognize that we have it, and work on it.

Through the healing meditations, I got many trapped emotions I didn't know I had out of my body. For example, someone mentioned the name Ofelia when I found this information. While doing one of the meditations, I remembered I had a nanny named Ofelia as a child. She cared for my sister and me when we were little because my parents worked. I remember when I was five years old, she didn't come back one day to care of us. I had a memory of her lovingly combing my hair, and it would always come to mind. After that, I don't have a memory of me running a comb through my hair growing up. I don't even remember having a comb. My mom used to cut my hair short; maybe it was so she didn't have to comb it because my hair was curly and hard to comb. As I'm writing this, tears are rolling down my cheeks. Back to the subject during the meditation, I remembered her. I began to cry desperately and said, "Ofelia, where is Ofelia? I don't want her to leave! I want Ofelia to come back!" I started crying like a five-year-old girl, weeping for Ofelia because they never told us she wasn't coming back and never gave me a chance to cry. She simply didn't come back one day. I had kept that feeling for many years, and that day I was able to get it out. I hope one day to see Ofelia again and thank her for the love she showed me.

While doing an exercise called "letting go of the parents" or forgiving them, I realized I had more masculine energy. I always believed I was like men by not using the restroom as often as women, and I always thought I got along better with men than women. After doing the exercise, at night, I started going to the restroom often times, which was unusual. The next day the same thing happened; it was like something was released in my body. I wondered what had happened to me, and while meditating on it, I realized that unconsciously I always wanted to be like a man because someone had told me that my parents didn't want me because I was born a female. So wanting to please my parents, I had that belief in my subconscious. Once I forgave my parents, I could take that emotional burden off myself. I don't know if what they told me is true, but we must be careful with what we say to our children; we can put emotional burdens on them without knowing it.

Another one of my problems was anxiety; I didn't know I had anxiety. When I found this information, I realized I was always in the "fight and flight" response mode. Which is an automatic psychological response of the body to a stressful or panic situation, which activates the sympathetic nervous system and triggers a response of stress that prepares the body for fight or flight. I was always aware of my surroundings to be ready if something bad happened, but I didn't know it was anxiety. Rather, I didn't know what it was like not to have anxiety; I had lived my whole life with anxiety. It affected my work because I always doubted myself and thought I had done everything wrong. I had just lived, always catastrophizing.

I could feel the adrenaline or feeling of fear and anxiety like a warm liquid running through my body. While working on myself and thinking about why this would happen to me, I realized that it was because I didn't have confidence in myself and felt incapable. As a child, I never received praise. I didn't have someone tell me I had done things well, so when I was older, I always doubted my abilities and capabilities at work. When I started to change myself and change my negative thoughts to positive thoughts, little by little, I began to feel calm and realized I had anxiety. And now, I put in my head that I'm capable, and I'm still working on.

What also helped me was the advice of my Bioemotion Therapist, Sandra Llaguno. She recommended that I concentrate on doing only one thing at a time and live in the present because I always multitask to avoid wasting time. But that only caused me more anxiety. When I started concentrating on doing one thing at a time, I realized that I had lived with anxiety my whole life. And now, I can tell when I have anxiety because now I know what it feels like not to have it. And now, I can do something to control my anxiety when I feel like I have it. What also helped was not to think so much about the past and live in the present. That has helped me tremendously because what happened already happened, and the future hasn't happened, so living in the present is the best thing you can do.

CHAPTER 10
EVERYTHING IS PERFECT

Finally, I want to talk to you about the vibrations in our bodies. I added an illustration of the Hertz vibration scale for you to see. Our vibrations depend on our mood. The lowest vibrations are pride, fear, guilt, and shame. Among the highest vibrations are love, happiness, and peace. That is why the Bible, in Galatians 5:22, tells us about these emotions we must cultivate. And what happens when we are vibrating at the lowest levels? We attract precarious situations, scarcity, and the like. And on the contrary, when we vibrate at the highest, good things come to us.

When we are thinking negative thoughts, we are vibrating at low frequencies. An example of negative thinking would be, "I'm afraid that something will happen to me," "I'm afraid that something will happen to my children, my husband, my parents," or "I'm afraid I won't be able to make ends meet." There are thousands of negative thoughts we can think of, but to vibrate at the highest levels, we have to think the opposite. Think positive thoughts to vibrate at high frequencies like "I am grateful for everything I have at this moment, my life, my health, and my children." Or "I'm happy with what I have," "when I pay for something, I pay it with pleasure because what I get in return is good for me," and so on. Earlier, I told you about intuition, we

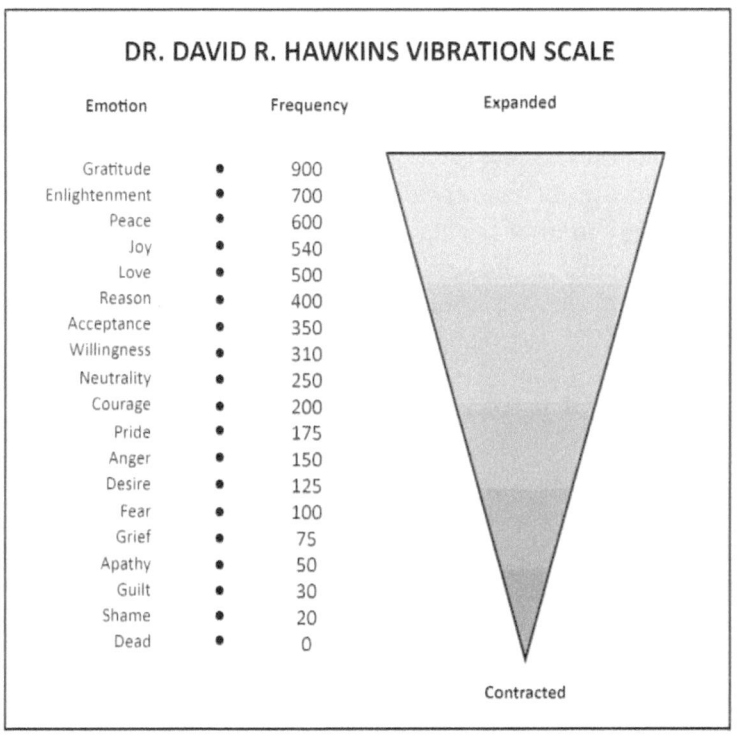

DR. DAVID R. HAWKINS VIBRATION SCALE

Emotion		Frequency	Expanded
Gratitude	•	900	
Enlightenment	•	700	
Peace	•	600	
Joy	•	540	
Love	•	500	
Reason	•	400	
Acceptance	•	350	
Willingness	•	310	
Neutrality	•	250	
Courage	•	200	
Pride	•	175	
Anger	•	150	
Desire	•	125	
Fear	•	100	
Grief	•	75	
Apathy	•	50	
Guilt	•	30	
Shame	•	20	
Dead	•	0	

Contracted

can feel the intentions or feelings of others, and they affect us. I will give examples of how that intuition or instinct can affect others. In the first example, there are two brothers. One of them has resentment against his father because he mistreated him or for any other reason. And the other brother perceives his brother's intention against his father, so although he loves his brother because he is his brother, he treats him with contempt. All this is happening, and they are not aware of it. The second example; is a son who despises his mother because she harbors resentment toward his father. The mother resents her husband because maybe he mistreats her, cheats on her with another woman, or for other reasons. The son picks up on the mother's intention and treats her with contempt. Again, they are unaware of the situation; the parents only see the son acting rebellious.

In the last example, let me tell you that children can feel their parents' intentions toward them, although they don't tell them. They can sense when there is a feeling of rejection, envy, or resentment on the part of one of the parents against the child. Maybe because the parent thinks it is the child's fault, he can no longer have fun after having the child, or because he didn't want to have the child in the first place and is angry at him. When this happens, the children rebel against their parents. The parents blame the child for being rebellious but don't know they are causing the problem. And when the father or the mother changes their intention toward their child, the child will change automatically. So be careful of your feelings towards your children or other people. Neutralize those bad motivations, meaning try not to feel anything, good or bad, against the person who did you wrong or is causing discomfort. You will see how the situation changes without even saying anything.

Learn to accept the situations that come your way as something good for you. They may sometimes not be so pleasant, but you will realize after it was the best for you. Everything is perfect. Sometimes we don't like change and don't want to accept it, but life gives them to us to learn. You will always get something good out of those situations, and this learning will train you or prepare you for other challenges in life. When you let go and trust, everything is better.

When you face any situation with optimism, you will always save yourself from unnecessary burdens and suffering. For example, a family's father may lose his job, or a single mother may lose her job. The person has two options: feel bad, feel like a failure, feel like a victim of the situation, and have problems at home for the same reason. Or they can think positively and trust that something good is coming their way. While they look for another job, they can make better use of their time. Like, enjoying every moment they spend with their family, working on themselves by taking courses, making some changes in the home, or things like that. I'm not saying the person won't be sad or worried; that is normal. Still, they shouldn't be sad to the point of hopelessness because they will most likely find a job, and if not, we know that God never abandoned us. Hence the saying, "God squeezes but doesn't choke." The person will realize that after that situation has passed. If they don't take advantage of their time off in the best way possible, they will beat themselves up later for not doing so before returning to work.

Everything is perfect; all the situations we face are for our good and to learn something. Even when we meet people who hurt us, they are there to teach us something, and we have to be grateful they came into our lives, honor them, and wish them the best. It sounds a bit strange; you may think, "there were terrible people who harmed me, and I want them to pay for what they did to me." There is a reason why they came into our lives; they taught us something, as we read in the chapter on the wounds of the soul. But don't worry; once you fully understand this and practice it, it will not be difficult to understand this concept, and you will know it's for your good. You have more to gain than to lose by practicing acceptance and forgiveness. If you don't do it for the other person, do it for yourself, so you can live in peace. Doing all this takes time and seeing results too, but it's well worth it.

Learn to forgive and love all people, which is why our creator tells us, "we must love our neighbor as ourselves." So learn to love everyone, even your enemies; they are teaching you something. It's the best thing you can do in your life. Holding a grudge and resentment only brings you illness. Putting this into practice is quite a process, but only by practicing what you learn, and over time you will see the results. If you practice it, you will see that only good and positive things will come into your life. But everything happens for our greatest good.

I want to make clear that I don't hold resentment against my biological parents, my adoptive parents, or my grandfather. It's clear they were also affected by someone else. I thank them for my life, and the experiences lived because, despite everything, my tragic start in this world, and being destined to fail, I did it; I made it. I got to where I am today.

Although my brother Johnny was not as lucky as me, he was also given away by my parents. But he could never attend school, have a house, and was abused as a child. I tried to help him many times, but at the time, I didn't have the knowledge I have today, and I couldn't quite understand his problems. In the year 2021, I wanted to buy a house for him to live in because I felt something terrible was going to happen. I wanted to teach him everything I was learning, but it couldn't happen for one reason or another. My brother and his tragic fate hurt me so much. Unfortunately, in January 2022, he was killed. Now he rests in peace, and I know that although he also hurt others with his death, he paid for his sins and the damage he caused to others. Now he no longer lives tormented by what they did to him or by what he did to others.

Most people have grown up with childhood trauma and need to heal. Of course, not all of them will recognize it, but those that do recognize it still have time to heal. I hope you have understood that by overcoming your traumas, you will think more clearly, make better decisions and do better in life. Try to raise your level of consciousness, meaning be more aware of yourself and your feelings, take care of your body and the planet, and just feel love and good vibes towards all people.

Practice giving; give of your time and resources, even if you think you don't have anything to offer. We all have something to give. When you give, it returns to you multiplied, be grateful for everything, and with everyone, especially our creator, always give thanks for how much or how little you have. You will see how your life changes for the better. Jesus said, "there is more happiness in giving than there is in receiving" in Acts 20:35.

Don't judge people; you are nobody to judge others. Only our creator has the right to do so. When we say, "I feel sorry for that person," we are already judging them because we think they can't get ahead on their own. When we say "that person is a stuck-up" because he is rich because he went to college, or for whatever reason, we are already judging them. Whenever you feel tempted to judge others, use and repeat this Gestalt prayer or poem by Psychotherapist Fritz Perls: "I am I. You are you. I'm not in this world to meet your expectations. You are not in this world to fulfill mine."

Never care about what other people say, never worry about what they will say, it doesn't matter, as long as you accept yourself, that's enough. You don't need the approval of others. Don't let your happiness depend on other people. Just do the best you can.

Never use the words "I am afraid of" because whatever you fear will happen to you. I tell you from experience everything I have been afraid of has happened to me. Remove the word "fear" from your mind unless it's a real threat, so it's good to feel afraid and act accordingly to save your life.

Live in the present, just learn from the past, and don't worry about the future. 80% of what we think is going to happen doesn't happen. Of the 20% remaining, things don't happen as we had imagined, so why spend time and energy on something that will not happen?

Use afformations to create a different life for yourself. Up until now, you have been using the afformations incorrectly. Instead of asking yourself, why I'm not doing well in life? Ask yourself, why do I do well, and I'm I successful? Why do I find a job I like? Why do I find a partner who loves and respects me? Depending on your concern, ask yourself these questions every day until you believe them.

Do you want to be successful in life? Just remember that "success" is not measured in money, but rather success is a state of mind. You are successful when you are truly happy, and you can do whatever you want when you want without anything stopping you.

You can do everything you want, and you set your mind to do in this world since God has given you that ability. But if you think you can, then you are correct, but if you think you can't, you are also correct, says Henry Ford. It costs the same to think positively than to think negatively; you decide. Repeat this when going through any unfavorable situation or resisting a situation: "I let go and trust" because everything happens for your greatest good, even bad things.

As I said before, my intention in writing this book is to help others. I hope that everything I have shared with you has helped you wake up, be more aware of your personality, and help you live a more calm and more peaceful life. Always do everything out of love. Get rid of fear, resentment, hate, anger, guilt, jealousy, hostility, the desire to hurt others, and anything else that doesn't let you move forward. And learn to forgive. The more you practice this, the better your life will be. Some people have a desire to hurt others and feel pleasure when they do it, but since they have done it for so long no longer realize they are doing it. Have you ever wondered why you don't have friends? This could be the reason.

Have only positive thoughts in your mind. Thinking positive things is following the advice of our creator, and he is never wrong. He tells us in Philippians 4:8, "whatever things are true, whatever things are of serious concern, whatever things are righteous... whatever things are lovable… continue considering these things." It is simple advice, but it could change our lives if we take it and practice it.

Don't let your past define your future; you can write your own destiny every day with your positive thoughts and actions. Remember, everything is perfect. I wish you the best on your journey toward your healing.

Thank you for reading my book, and if you know someone who can benefit from it, please share it with them. I hope this book has helped you be more aware of yourself, your emotions, and your environment. The last thing I can tell you is that love can conquer anything, "love never fails," as 1 Corinthians 13:8 says. Love helps us to be better people. As long as we do everything out of love, everything will be all right, and everything good will come to us.

ABOUT THE AUTHOR

Originally from Mexico, Dahlia Quiñonez has lived in Southern California most of her life. She studied Business Administration at the University of California Irvine, Extension, and Accounting and Finance at Santa Ana College.

She has owned several businesses since 2012. She currently owns Dalia's Travel Agency, which led her to write the book "How to Become a Travel Agent" to help other people take up this noble career. She is also a Health Insurance Agent since 2016 and a Real Estate Agent.

She is a philanthropist who has volunteered with various non-profit organizations that help women and small businesses. She has served as Director of Community Relations at ALPFA, the Association of Latino Professionals for America. A non-profit organization that helps empower and develop Latino men and women as leaders of character for the nation in all sectors of the global community.

Currently, she serves as a Community Ambassador for the non-profit organization Orange County SCORE. A resource partner of the SBA, the U.S. Small Business Administration, which offers free and low-cost business mentoring and training, as well as numerous resources and tools to help start or grow a business. She has also volunteered at WHW, Women Helping Women. A non-profit organization that provides the unemployed and underemployed with the skills and resources they need to get and keep a good job.

She loves to travel, exercise, and enjoy nature. You can connect with Dahlia at www.awakendespertar.com or on her social media, on Instagram as @awakendespertarbook.

Follow me on my other ventures:

Follow me on my other ventures:
www.daliastravel.com
www.dahliarealtor.com
www.youtube.com/awakendespertarbook
www.tiktok.com/awakenbook
wwww.instagram.com/awakendespertarbook
www.facebook.com/dahlia.quinonez
www.facebook.com/dahliaqrealtor
www.linkedin.com/dahliaquinonez
www.facebook.com/dqmedicareinsuranceagent

Books I recommend you read:

The Six Pillars of Self-esteem. Nathaniel Branden
Breaking the Habit of Being Yourself. Joe Dispenza.
Your Child, Your Mirror. Martha Alicia Chavez
Enjoy Life Forever! Watch Tower & Tract Society of Pennsylvania. www.jw.org.

Please remember to leave a review on the platform you bought the book; this will help me spread the word about the book, and more people can read it.

Terms:

Love bombing: Love bombing is the practice of showing a person excessive affection and attention as a way of manipulating them in a relationship. The term is most commonly used in a negative way in the context of individuals who use it on romantic partners (or desired romantic partners) or cult members who use it as a recruitment technique. Love bombing typically takes the form of showering a person with a combination of seemingly genuine expressions of love or attention, such as excessive praise, gifts, and grand gestures. In love bombing, this behavior goes beyond the heightened level of attention that can be common at the beginning of relationships. It is thought to be part of a pattern of emotionally abusive behavior in which it is done to socially isolate and control a person by making them emotionally and socially dependent on the manipulator. After the manipulator gains a level of control, they often become distant and begin to engage in other forms of emotional abuse, such as gaslighting (dictionary.com).

Codependency: In sociology, **codependency** is a theory that attempts to explain imbalanced relationships where one person enables another person's self-destructive behavior such as addiction, poor mental health, immaturity, irresponsibility, or under-achievement. Definitions of codependency vary, but typically include high self-sacrifice, a focus on others' needs, suppression of one's own emotions, and attempts to control or fix other people's problems. People who self-identify as codependent exhibit low self-esteem, but it is unclear whether this is a cause or an effect of characteristics associated with codependency. Codependency is not limited to married, partnered, or romantic relationships, as co-workers, friends, and family members can be codependent as well (Wikipedia.org).

Empathy: Empathy is the ability to recognize, understand, and share the thoughts and feelings of another person, animal, or fictional character. Developing empathy is crucial for establishing relationships and behaving compassionately. It involves experiencing another person's point of view, rather than just one's own, and enables prosocial or helping behaviors that come from within, rather than being forced (Psychologytoday.com).

Gaslighting: Gaslighting is a form of psychological abuse in which a person or group causes someone to question their own sanity, memories, or perception of reality. People who experience gaslighting may feel confused, anxious, or as though they cannot trust themselves. (medicalnewstoday.com)

Histrionic: Histrionic personality disorder (HPD) is defined by the American Psychiatric Association as a personality disorder characterized by a pattern of excessive attention-seeking behaviors, usually beginning in early childhood, including inappropriate seduction and an excessive desire for approval. People diagnosed with the disorder are said to be lively, dramatic, vivacious, enthusiastic, extroverted and flirtatious. People with HPD have a high desire for attention, make loud and inappropriate appearances, exaggerate their behaviors and emotions, and crave stimulation. Associated features include egocentrism, self-indulgence, continuous longing for appreciation, and persistent manipulative behavior to achieve their own wants (Wikipedia.org).

Leveling: Leveling refers to the disturbed character's attempt to put himself on equal standing with others of different character. It generally takes two forms: setting oneself up as a person of equal stature to a person in authority; and trying to equate one's own character, personal value, integrity, etc. with someone else's, especially one of more mature or superior character. Leveling is a slick way to try and "level the playing field" or field of interpersonal contest. Example: a woman confronting her husband about his frequent displays of verbal abuse. She stated: "I'd like you to simply ask me for what you need instead of launching into me, cursing, and berating me. When I want something from you, I ask for it." His retort, in a very provocative tone: "Are you saying you're better than me?" The implied message he was sending was that the two of them were of equal character standing — just two human beings of equal worth. He was also implying that the wife was being demanding or "uppity" by challenging him to do things differently (and insinuating that her way was better than his way). The woman in the above example may or may not have been familiar with the tenets of classical psychology or the many commonly accepted beliefs that flow from it, but she was definitely vulnerable to the tactic. Instead of thinking to herself, "This is just another way he's trying to take the wind out of my sails and put me in my place," she thought, "Maybe I am putting him down and of course I don't mean to imply that I'm better than he is, so I'll back off." So, in the end, she did just as he wanted and the tactic worked (counsellingresource.com

Fight & Flight: The fight-or-flight or the fight-flight-or-freeze response (also called hyperarousal or the acute stress response) is a physiological reaction that occurs in response to a perceived harmful event, attack, or threat to survival. It was first described by Walter Bradford Cannon. His theory states that animals react to threats with a general discharge of the sympathetic nervous system, preparing the animal for fighting or fleeing (dbpedia.org).

Empath: Empaths are highly sensitive individuals, who have a keen ability to sense what people around them are thinking and feeling. Psychologists may use the term empath to describe a person that experiences a great deal of empathy, often to the point of taking on the pain of others at their own expense (Psychalive.org).

REFERENCES

Page iii, 36, 76, and 88
All Bible references were taken from the New World Translation of the Holy Scriptures online at www.jw.org. None of the information or opinions in this book were taken from there.
Page 2
Por el Placer de Vivir. Cesar Lozano, Dr. Cesarlozano.com
Page 5
Definition of Trauma by SanaMente.org.
Page 6
Definition of trauma due to physical abuse by wikipedia.org.
Page 7
Definition of trauma due to sexual abuse by pepsic.bvsalud.org.
Page 8
Description of the consequences derived from sexual violence by the Secretariat Against Sexual Violence, Exploitation and Human Trafficking of the Government of Guatemala (www.svet.gob.gt).
Page 9-10
Post-traumatic stress trauma description by Medlineplus.gov.
Page 11
Physical or psychological and emotional abuse trauma description by Wikipedia.org.
Page 12, 13
Emotional Abandonment trauma description by Wikipedia.org.
Page 14
Personality Disorder description by Mayoclinic.org.
Page 16, 17
Paranoid Personality Disorder description by Medlineplus.org.
Page 17
Schizoid Personality Disorder description by Mayoclinic.org.
Page 18
Schizotypal Personality Disorder description by Mayoclinic.org.
Page 19-21
Antisocial Personality Disorder description by Mayoclinic.org.
Page 21-23
Borderline Personality Disorder description by Mayoclinic.org.
Page 23, 24
Histrionic Personality Disorder description by Medlineplus.gov.
Page 24-27
Narcissistic Personality Disorder description by Mayoclinic.org.
Page 27
Avoidant Personality Disorder description by Medlineplus.gov.

REFERENCES

Page 28
Dependent Personality description by Medlineplus.org.
Page 29
Obsessive-Compulsive Personality Disorder description by Medlineplus.gov.
Page 31
Dissociative Identity Disorder description by Mayoclinic.org.
Page 32
Split movie by director M. Night Shyamalan. HBO documentary "Multiple Personalities." Encina Severa, YouTuber. www.youtube.com/c/encinasevera
Page 34
Cleaning Up Your Mental Mess. Caroline Leaf, Neurocientist. drleaf.com
Page 35
The five wounds that prevent you from being yourself, Liz Bourbeau. Lisebourbeau.com
Page 36, 69
Tom Nuyens, Alive Academy. alive-academy.com
Finding your Roots. pbs.org
Page 48, 61
Christane Northrup, Dr. drnorthrup.com
Fernando Leiva, Psychologist. YouTube Channel Noche de Psicoterapia.
Page 53
Ramani Duvursula, Dr. doctor–ramani.com
Page 62, 67
Amor Zero and Familia Zero, Iñaki Piñuel, Dr. Inakipinuel.com. Traumatic Bond description by MedicalNewsToday.com.
Page 67
Nicky 69
Forgiving Yourself and Others. Carolle Jean-Murat, Dr. drcarolle.com
Page 71
Raynor College of Massage & Natural Therapy. Raynormassage.com
Aaron T. Beck, Dr. Founder of the Cognitive Behavioral Therapy(CBT). Beckisntitute.org
Page 74
Virtual EMDR Therapy. You can find it by going to bit.ly/3vbgYAL. Click on "start your free trial."
Page 81
Sandra Llaguno, Bioemotion Therapist. sandrallaguno.com
Page 83
Vibration scale by Dr. David R. Hawkins.
Page 87
Gestalt Prayer/Poem by Pyschoterapist Fritz Perls y Laura Perls.
Page 90

REFERENCES

ALPFA, alpfa.org. SCORE, orangecounty.score.org. Women Helping Women, Irvine, CA.

Photos by Maryori Photography. Facebook.com/maryoriphotograpy
Ilustrations by Charly López. Facebook.com/charlylópezdibujanteartistico.
Book cover designed by James Whites. Fivver.com

www.ingramcontent.com/pod-product-compliance
Lightning Source LLC
Chambersburg PA
CBHW020323130626
46549CB00003B/994